The Robe of Sins

And A Crown Of Thorns

Janice M. H. Brown

Copyright © 2018 by Janice M. H. Brown

All rights reserved
Rejoice Essential Publishing
P.O. BOX 512
Effingham, SC 29541
www.republishing.org

All rights reserved. No part of this book may be used or reproduced by any means, graphics, electronic, or mechanical, including photocopying, recording, taping, or by any information storage retrieval system without the written permission of the publisher except in the case of brief Quotations embodied in critical articles and reviews.

Scripture quotations marked (NIV) are taken from the Holy Bible, New International Version ®, NIV®. Copy-right © 1973, 1978, 1984, 2011 by Biblica, Inc.™ Used by permission of Zondervan. All rights reserved.

Scripture quotations marked (NKJV) are taken from the New King James Version®. Copyright © 1982 by Thomas Nelson. Used by permission. All rights reserved.

Scripture quotations taken from the New American Standard Bible® (NASB), Copyright © 1960, 1962, 1963, 1968, 1971, 1972, 1973, 1975, 1977, 1995 by The Lockman Foundation Used by permission. www.Lockman.org

Scripture quotations taken from the Amplified Bible (AMPC) Copyright © 1954, 1958, 1962, 1964, 1965, 1987 by The Lockman Foundation Used by permission. www.Lockman.org

Scripture quotations marked (NLT) are taken from the Holy Bible, New Living Translation, copyright ©1996, 2004, 2015 by Tyndale House Foundation. Used by permission of Tyndale House Publishers, Inc., Carol Stream, Illinois 60188. All rights reserved.

Scripture quotations marked (ESV) are taken from the Holy Bible, English Standard Version® (ESV®) Copyright ©2001 by Crossway, a publishing ministry of Good News Publishers. All rights reserved.

Scriptures marked as "(GNT)" are taken from the Good News Translation- Second Edition © 1992 by American Bible Society. Used by permission.

Unless otherwise indicated, scripture is taken from the King James Version

The Robe Of Sins/Janice M. H. Brown

ISBN-10: 1-946756-38-5
ISBN-13: 978-1-946756-38-1
Library of Congress Control Number: 2018956842

Dedication

The first dedication of this book goes to Jesus Christ, our Lord and Savior, who has stuck by me through all the storms, hills and valleys—making ways out of no way. Father, you know me better than anyone does. And I thank you for watching over me, keeping me close to you and never leaving my side. In 2006, after going through a life-threatening illness, I remember asking God, "Lord, what do you want me to do for you with this life you blessed me with?" That very night, I fell into a deep peaceful sleep. I dreamed of a bright light shining on a black Holy Bible with gold binding. The Bible was held up to my face, and the pages began to turn, stopping on the scriptures Matthew 10:9-20. The scriptures were high-lighted and lifted up from the pages. I will never forget that calling and I am on this battlefield! I am your servant and I am not afraid to do what you say do and to go where you say go. God's word tells me that 'thou art with me always!' According to Matthew 28:20, God's word says, "Teaching them (new disciples) to observe all things whatsoever I have commanded you; and, lo, I am with you always, even unto the end of the world. Amen." Thank you, Jesus, for allowing me to continue to serve you and to be observant to your words. I love you so much!

The second dedication of this book goes to Prentis Brown Jr., my wonderful husband, best friend, and partner. Thank you for your encouragement, abundance of support, your patience and listening ears to the many open visions that God shared with me throughout my journey. You are one of my biggest blessings! Thank you for so much laughter, and the wonderful unconditional love you have always displayed to me during our many years of marriage and the writing of this wonderful book. Words cannot begin to explain how honored I feel to have you as my husband and the head of our house. Thanks for being a man after God's own heart! I love you!

The third dedication of this book goes to my precious son Prentis Brown III, for always making time for your mother regardless of whatever you are doing, and for being a good son and making motherhood look easy! As I watch God continue to give you favor, my heart warms over with so much joy. Just recently, he blessed you with a beautiful and loving wife, Mrs. Victoria Boykins-Brown. We love our daughter-in law very much, she's such a blessing and a wonderful addition to the family! I thank God for blessing you with the many talents and skills that have truly helped support many of my projects through the years to include this wonderful book. Many thanks for your contributions! I love you!

Contents

ACKNOWLEDGMENT xvii

PREFACE..xxiii

INTRODUCTION..1

CHAPTER 1:   What Is Sin?...............8

CHAPTER 2:   Types of Sins............19

CHAPTER 3:   Levels of Sins............33

CHAPTER 4:   Who Committed The First Sin?...................45

CHAPTER 5:   Punishment for Sins And Disobeying God.........57

CHAPTER 6:   The First Sacrifice to Cover The First Sin......................60

CHAPTER 7:   How Sin Affects our Relationship with God...................64

CHAPTER 8: The Robe of Sins Word Listing and Scriptures...................69

ABOMINABLE 70

ABUSE...72

ACCUSATIONS 73

ADDICTION..75

ADULTERY..77

AFFLICTION...79

ANGER...81

ANGUISH...83

ANXIETY...85

BACKSLIDER..87

BETRAY..89

BITTERNESS..90

BLASPHEMY...91

BOAST..93

BONDAGE...95

BURDEN..96

CHEATER..97

COMPLAINER..99

CONDEMNATION...101

CONFUSION..102

CORRUPTION	104
COVETOUS	106
CRIME	108
CRITICIZING	109
CROOKED	111
CURSING	113
DEATH	115
DECEITFUL	117
DEFEAT	119
DEFILE	121
DELUSION	123
DEPRAVITY	124
DESPAIR	126
DESPERATE	127
DESPISE	128
DESTRUCTION	130
DISAPPOINTMENT	132
DISCOURAGE	134
DISOBEDIENCE	135
DISTRESS	137
DIVISION	140
DOUBLE-MINDEDNESS	141
DOUBT	143

DRUNKENNESS..145

EFFEMINATE..147

ENEMIES. 149

ENTICE..151

ENVY..153

EVILDOER..155

EXTORTION...157

FAILURE..158

FALSE WITNESS..160

FEAR...162

FOOLISHNESS..164

FORNICATION..166

FRAUD...168

FRUSTRATION...170

GAMBLING...172

GOSSIP..174

GREED..176

GRIEF..179

GRUDGE..181

GUILT...182

HARASMENT..184

HATE..185

HEARTACHE..187

HEARTBREAK	188
HOMOSEXUALITY	190
HYPOCRITE	192
IDOL	194
IGNORANCE	196
IMMORALITY	198
INJUSTICE	200
INSANITY	202
INTIMIDATION	204
JEALOUSY	205
LAZINESS	207
LIAR	209
LOSS	211
LUST	213
MALICE	215
MANIPULATION	216
MASTURBATION	218
MISERY	220
MOCKERY	221
MISTAKE	222
MURDER	224
NEGLECT	226
OCCULTISM	228

OFFEND	230
OPPRESSION	231
PAIN	233
PERSESCUTION	235
POVERTY	236
PREJUDICE	238
PRESSURE	240
PRIDE	241
PROSTITUTION	243
PROVOKE	245
PUNISHMENT	247
RAGE	249
REBELLIOUS	250
REGRET	252
REJECTION	254
RESENTMENT	256
REVENGE	258
SADNESS	260
SATANIC	261
SELFISHNESS	264
SELF-RIGHTEOUSNESS	266
SHAME	268
SICKNESS	270

SLANDER..272

SLOTH...274

SORROW...276

STEAL...277

STRESS...278

STRIFE..280

SUFFER...281

SUICIDE..283

SWEAR...285

TEMPTATION..287

TERRORISM..289

THIEVES...291

THREATS..292

TORMENT...294

TRANSGRESSION...................................296

TREPASS..297

UNFAITHFUL..298

UGLY..300

UNBELIEF...302

UNFORGIVENESS...................................304

UNGODLY...306

UNRIGHTEOUSNESS...............................308

VANITY..310

VIOLENCE..312
VOODOO..314
WHORE...315
WICKED..317
WITCHCRAFT..319
WOE...321
WORRY..323
WORTHLESSNESS...325
ADDITIONAL SCRIPTURES.........................327
ABOUT THE AUTHOR....................................329
INDEX..340
REFERENCES...345

Acknowledgments

To my parents, first, my late mother Eldress Katie Leigh Nancy Cooper Horne, thank you mama, for your words of wisdom. A stubborn child I was, but your words of wisdom still ring in my ears — "Janice, you can't live in this world alone baby." Those words fell from your lips so kind, so gentle, and so tenderly. But when they fell on my heart, they fell like a ton of bricks crushing that wall of stubbornness in my heart into pieces so small that you can't even find a trace of it. I remember when the tears broke from my eyes, crying myself into a hic-cup state. It was then when I began to learn to love and found myself capable of letting others into my heart. Love you and I miss you dear mother!

Thank you to my dear father, Deacon William Henry Horne Sr. for always ready and willing to impart so much wisdom and knowledge. You are truly a stand-up dad, raising ten children; surely, that could not have been easy for you, we didn't have much, but you made sure we had a roof over our head and food to eat. We had tough times, fun times, but most of all memorable times. Thank you both for my first layer of foundation in Jesus Christ so that I might be rooted and grounded in Him. Words cannot express how much both of you are loved and appreciated!

To my mother-in-law Elder Sarah Brown and father-in-law, the late Elder Prentis Brown Sr., thank you for our many Bible discussions and for being an excellent example of a strong and godly family. I love you! Miss you Daddy Brown!

Thank you to my spiritual mother and father, Christina King and Alvin King, for pouring into my life the spirit of love, kindness, wisdom and always lifting me and my family up in prayer! Much love to you both!

Before I go in any further, I would like to acknowledge my best friend, Janet A. Love. During our time we spent in Misawa Japan, as the newest and the youngest Director in our group, I was forever taking notes, always a pen in hand. It was twenty-one years ago when you began teasing me and encouraged me to "write that book."

I've lost count of the many times you had my back and showed me that unconditional sisterly love. Always a big sister! You have truly lived up to your last name. I love you and thank you, Janet. Our friendship means more to me than you'll ever know!

Thank you to my dear friend and sister-in-Christ, Kimberly A. Grisson, for your overwhelming and generous support in helping make this book possible. Your kind deed is greatly appreciated. Love you sister!

A special thank you to my niece Charmekia Bias, for being creative in my Author Photo of "The Robe of Sins" from (CharMarie Photography). Your hard work is greatly appreciated. Much love!

A special thank you to Apostle Rosa Martin, for hearing God's voice and allowing God to use you and being obedience to His words in guiding and encouraging me to write this book. I love you and appreciate you! May God continue to bless you!

Thank you to all the Spirit-filled Pastors and Ministers that have been spiritual fathers and mothers to our family. We consider ourselves truly blessed to have so many that spoke into our lives — Pastor, Bishop Paul Keeter & Doctor Lou Keeter; Pastor, Bishop Larry O. Wright Sr.; Pastor Virgil Reaves and Sister Phyllis Reaves; Pastor Elder Anthony Talmadge; the late Pastor K. P. Johnson; the late Minister Kathleen McClean; and the late Pastor Marion Wright! We love you all!

The late Sarah Brown Barnes (Vern), my dear sweet sister-in-law. Thank you for being obedient to God. Your wisdom and compassion have truly been a blessing. I appreciate everything you did for me and my family when I was on my sickbed recovering from breast cancer. You moved right in and you showed me love and kindness while you helped washed and cleaned my wounds. As you bandaged me up you prayed for me and talked with me. While Prentis and I was in our Valley, you climbed down in that Valley with us. You brought that calm, comforting spirit with you. You helped nurtured us back to health. You were a blessing to us. We drew from your strength. I miss our friendship sister! I remember you telling me that you loved me so much that you wished that I was a chocolate chip cookie so that you could dip me into a glass of milk and eat me up! Yum, Yum!! Oh, dear God! I am so fighting back tears right now! Oh, well I just lost that fight! You truly were like an angel walking among us. God clearly loved you best, because you are now with Him. We will always love you and we miss you dear Vern! May you rest in peace!

A special thank you to my book publisher, Rejoice Essential Publishing!! I appreciate all of your teams' hard work, from the cover designers, editors, marketing people, accountants, contract people, administrators and so on for pushing my book to be one of the best of its kind. Your professionalism and patience are a great credit to your company! God Bless!

Preface

In June 2012, my husband and I became Youth Directors in a small local church in Fayetteville, North Carolina. Our Pastor prayed over the Youth Department position before he shared with us that God had appointed us to these positions. We were so excited to head up the Youth Department. We held other positions in church, but this was the first time heading a Youth Department. After much prayer, we accepted the position. We prayed for God's guidance every step of the way. We did not want to let down God, the children, and the church.

We took this assignment very seriously. We knew that we wanted to do the very best for God, and to teach the children all about our Lord and Savior Jesus Christ. In Matthew 19:14 (NIV), Jesus tells us, "Let the little children come to me, and do not hinder them, for the kingdom of heaven belongs to such as these."

Having many years of experience of working with children from the age of infants to young adults made me feel very comfortable in this field. However, this assignment felt special, looking back at all the programs that I've started, headed and implemented, and for which I have received numerous awards. I've set up and managed other people's business as well as operated and owned a small business in Day Care for a couple of years. However, somehow, this task of heading up a church Youth Department felt different. We felt very privileged and honored to even have been asked to step into an important role such as this —to introduce Jesus Christ to our children! For some children, this was their first time ever hearing about Jesus! WOW! This was a big deal!

When my husband and I took on this assignment, the church class had about 3 children. A year into the program, our enrollment grew rapidly in every age group, which was truly a blessing.

We took ownership of the Youth Department to include all aspect of setting up a youth-oriented ministry, such as church curriculum, schedules, yearly calendars and events, etc. We put together a Youth Explosion event. We felt somewhat nervous because this was a first for us. We knew that a great deal of work went into putting together a large event such as this since that involved all youth in the surrounding communities. We knew first, we had to come up with a theme. We went to God in prayer and waited for an answer and he did provide one for us. He gave us a theme: "Take A Risk; DARE to Be Unique In Jesus."

So excited, we made contact with over 500 churches and we also partnered up with local churches, and businesses for fundraisers' coupon; we also had door prizes and free food for the event in return for free advertisements throughout Fayetteville, NC and the surrounding areas. We created publicity through Letters, Radio, TV Community Channels, Flyers, Word of Mouth, and all social media. The invitation read as followed: Greetings! We are daring YOU to take a Risk by Being Unique in Jesus! Go ahead! WE DARE YOU! We are daring you to participate in an exciting Youth Explosion event. This year, we have decided to do Sub-Themes, and we are daring you to incorporate your presentation according to one of our 10 Sub-Themes. The Presentation may be in a form of a Praise Dance, and/or bring pages of the Bible to life through Drama Plays, Short-Skit, Mime, Youth Choir, Rap Songs, and /Poem.

As I began to talk with God, I explained to Him that I needed to come up with something special for the children at the church, because they were the host of all of the children that would be coming from the other churches throughout the community.

The deeper I got into my word, the more I began to hear God's voice. There was a certain scripture that tugged at my heart, Habakkuk 2:2 (NIV), which says, "Then the LORD said to me, "Write my answer plainly on tablets, so that a runner can carry the correct message to others ."

God began to minister to me and He shared an open vision of a very special play, titled "A Shift In The Atmosphere" as well as songs and scriptures. He displayed the play before my very eyes from start to finish. Astonished at what I just saw, I began to write out everything that God told me to do. He began with the costumes, all of the costumes looked like those of biblical times except for the robe of Jesus Christ. I created the costumes just as He described them. Everything was so detailed. The play that He had me to write was very moving and powerful. It left the audience in tears of joy. There was a part in the play that portrayed Jesus Christ, and His robe was very unique. Of all the costumes I created, the robe to be worn by Jesus' character, stood out above all the rest.

"The Robe Of Sins"— This is how God described the robe to me. "Jesus' Robe is to be beige, khaki or sack-like material, with a golden rope-like cord to frame the V-shape collar neck and down the front of the robe where the robe is to be opened. The robe is to be sleeveless, ankle length, and loose fitting. At the front of the robe on the inside, sew in a hidden pocket at the beginning of the V-neck line to hold a small flashlight. While the stage is dark and while Jesus is hanging on the cross and just as Jesus is about to transition over (or a Shift In The Atmosphere), the flashlight is to be turned on to show the appearance of His face lit by the glory of God, to show that God is well pleased with His Son."

He began to give me a complete vision of this robe! More detailed! He displayed an open vision to me of the robe with words of each individual sin written in red paint to represent the blood that Jesus Christ shed (the blood of the holy lamb). He went on to describe the imitation stones in detail. "Select regular cardboard paper and cut each individual square cardboard paper according to the length of each word. Go to the dollar store, select several stone-like contact papers, the kind you would line the cabinet with. Cut each contact paper square one inch all-around of each individual matched word to the cardboard. Cover each strips of cardboard paper with the stone-like contact paper. Cover the cardboard front and back.

The reason for the stone-like paper was to give the physicality, the appearance of the weight or the heaviness of each stone. Hand write each word of sin on the imitation stones with red paint. Each stone is to be attached to the robe to represent each sin that Jesus had to carry." I began to write a list of sins that covered the robe. As God gave me a complete vision of the robe, I began to meditate on the robe and the placing of each word. I know that there are many sins that Jesus carried, but these are the words I saw on "The Robe Of Sins."

As I began to sketch out the robe and the words of the many sins on the robe, I felt a sudden sadness come over my whole being. My heart began to ache and beat faster, tears fell from my eyes, and my heart literally broke when I thought about how heavy it is to carry just one of these sins. I could not stop crying for my Savior Jesus Christ because He carried all of them. All of our sins, He put them on like a robe, so that we may have everlasting life. And they beat Him to a bloody pulp while He carried our sins to the cross! I paused for a moment, thanking and praising our awesome God and meditating on Him and His Son, our Savior Jesus Christ. What an AWESOME GOD HE IS! God loves us so much, that He gave His ONLY Son for us (John 3:16 KJV). I really felt that I did not deserve to be loved like this. There is no greater love than this!

As I continued to write out the words on the robe, again I found myself sobbing uncontrollably, because I knew that many of the words written on this robe I was guilty of committing some of these very acts. Asking God to give me strength to write these words, immediately, I could feel the Holy Spirit taking over. My head quickly dropped to my chest and instantly I repented! My heart grew heavy as I began to self-convict. I asked God to forgive me for all the sins I did and I knew I was wrong, and to forgive me for the sins I committed and was unaware of. Each word I was guilty of felt like a dagger straight to my heart and Jesus' heart.

I remember thinking Paul must have felt like this when he wrote in Romans 7:15-20 (NIV), "I do not understand what I do. For what I want to do I do not do, but what I hate I do. And if I do what I do not want to do. I agree that the law is good. As it is, it is no longer I myself who do it, but it is sin living in me. For I know that good itself does not dwell in me, that is, in my sinful nature, For I have the desire to do what is good, but I cannot carry it out. For I do not do the good I want to do, but, the evil I do not want to do—this I keep on doing. Now if I do what I do not want to do, it is no longer I who do it, but it is sin living in me that does it."

Just one sin is too much of a burden and way too heavy to carry. It has been written time and time again on how Jesus Christ died for our sins and how He carried our sins to the cross and shed His blood for our sins. God gave His only begotten Son so that we may have everlasting life. There have been many books written on this topic. Many have re-enacted Jesus carrying that old rugged cross in many skits, plays and movies. Many robes and other costumes were created, depicted and worn by the actors; however, I have never seen anyone wear a robe quite like this one. When you really look at this robe and think about what it represents, or how one person could endure and carry all the world's sin on His shoulder, it is not only amazing, but it truly takes your breath away.

Bondage
Curse
Vanity
Terror
Hostility
Malice
Defeated
Slander
Distress
Disappointment
Bitterness
Cursing
Hate
Wicked
Revenge
Guilt
Fear
Coercion
Oppression
Spite
Heartbreak
Burden
Manipulation
Rages
Liar
Torment
Condemnation
Disobedience
Disrespectful
Murder
Immorality
Offend
Heartache
Pride
Trespass
Ignorance
Neglect
Provoke

Introduction

The scripture 1 Peter 5:7 (NIV) says, "Cast all your anxiety on him, because he cares for you." This scripture captures the essence of the title —The Robe Of Sins. When Jesus Christ put on our sins, He wore it like a Robe of Sins, carried all of our sins to the cross while being beaten and abused. He loved us so much when He did that; He laid it all at the cross and gave us mercy—we do nothing ourselves. "God made him who had no sin to be sin for us, so that in him we might become the righteousness of God" (2 Corinthians 5:21 NIV).

The words you speak out of your mouth help shape your life and future. The foundation of your life can be set by your words. When we speak or allow negative words to flow through our mind, we are setting up a boundary for ourselves that limits or hinders our growth in life and Christ. We need to realize and understand that our words are powerful. We speak life or death into our conditions, situations and or circumstances. God's word tells us that "life and death is in the tongue" (Proverbs 18:20-21), "A man's belly shall be satisfied with the fruit of his mouth; and with the increase of his lips shall he be filled. Death and life are in the power of the tongue: and they that love it shall eat the fruit thereof."

As you read some of the scriptures below, you can see God's Word has a lot to say about the words we speak over ourselves.

Proverb 18:7 — A fool's mouth is his destruction, and his lips are the snare of his soul.

Proverbs 15:4 — A wholesome tongue is a tree of life; but perverseness therein is a breach in the spirit.

Proverbs 21:23 — Whoso keepeth his mouth and his tongue keepeth his soul from troubles.

Proverbs 15:4 (AMPC) — A gentle tongue (with its healing power) is a tree of life, but willful contrariness in it breaks down the spirit.

Proverbs 16:23 — The heart of the wise teacheth his mouth, and addeth learning to his lips.

Proverbs 12:14 — A man should be satisfied with good by the fruit of his mouth: and the recompense of a man's hands shall be rendered unto him.

Job 22:28 — Thou shalt also decree a thing, and it shall be established unto thee: and the light shall shine upon thy ways.

Proverbs 16:24 — Pleasant words are as a honeycomb, sweet to the soul, and health to the bones.

There are many examples given throughout the Bible that support these scriptures. Here are a couple examples below:

In Mark 5:25-28, we see the woman with the issue of blood. Her words penetrated her spirit, "If I may touch but his clothes, I shall be whole." This woman spoke her healing into existence. She had hope and faith and she believed within her whole heart that she would be healed, and she was. Notice first that she spoke the word. She already had the hope, faith and belief, but then she put everything in ACTION by reaching out and touching Jesus' clothes; and it manifested her healing into existence.

In Romans 4:17, God changed Abram's name to Abraham, which means "father of nations." Even though Abraham knew he was old, he did not call himself old; instead, he called himself "father of nations." He believed in God and the words that God was telling him. Abraham spoke those things God promised him as though there were. As you can see, Abraham did become the father of many nations: "As it is written I have made thee a father of many nations, before him whom he believed, even God, who quickeneth the dead, and calleth those things which be not as though they were."

In 2 Timothy 1:7, we see another example. On a personal level, sharing a little of my testimony, I recalled in June 2006, when I was first diagnosed with breast cancer, I really don't ever remember being afraid. But I do remember thanking God for my healing and repeating it over and over again. Then a couple days later, it struck me all at once and I said to myself, "This is a serious matter! We are talking life and death! LORD, why am I not afraid?" God spoke to me and He said, "Because YOU know THAT I AM and because YOU will not STAY in this illness! YOU are only going through this! I need YOU to go through this, in order for me to get YOU where I need for YOU to be!"

This may sound silly, but I asked Him again, "But shouldn't I be afraid?" And then it seems like I felt God smiling down upon me and said, "YOU are going to be OK! UNDERSTAND, I did not give you the spirit of fear, but of power, and of love, and of a sound mind (2 Timothy 1:7)." I remember shaking my head up and down saying out loud, "OK GOD, I'm gonna TRUST YOU!" Now, you'd better believe that Satan came at me with everything that God allowed him to do. Satan hit me with every negative word that was ever associated with breast cancer. He created unbelievable situations for me that most people would have given up a long time ago. It was not easy, but I stayed positive, stayed the course, trusted God, and He did give me my healing! Not only that, He spared my life and made the old me, the new me. He saturated me with His fruit of the Spirit and THANK GOD, I don't look like what I've been through. And I give Him ALL THE GLORY AND THE HIGHEST PRAISE! Hallelujah!

We as Christian can carry that same attitude with us everywhere we go (hope, faith, belief and our action come by speaking positive words into our conditions, situations and/or circumstances). In other words, we need to be still and let God. And when we speak, we need to speak positiveness into the atmosphere and watch God work. He never fails.

CHAPTER 1

What Is Sin?

According to the Webster Dictionary, sin is "an immoral act considered to be a transgression against divine law; a sin in the eyes of God; wrong, wrongdoing, act of evil/wickedness, transgression, crime, offense, misdeed, misdemeanor; etc."

According to the Bible, it defined sin in the original translation as, "to miss the mark," that is, the standard of perfection established by God and evidenced by Jesus.

The Bible also tells us in 1 John 3:4, "Whoever committed sin transgresseth also the law: For sin is the transgression of the law."

As Jesus continued to teach me about "The Robe Of Sins," my eyes became more opened about sin. I don't believe that we are aware of the weight that each sin carries. However, we do know that each sin is a burden and very heavy to carry. Sin affects our everyday living in one way or another. What gives us comfort is to know that according to God's word in 1 Peter 5:7, we can "Cast all your anxiety on Him because he cares for you."

For me, this scripture captures the essence of "The Robe Of Sins." This scripture brings a sense of comfort knowing that whatever situation may be going on in our life big or small, there is nothing in this world too complicated or impossible for God to handle. When we sincerely cast all our cares upon Him, He takes it away from us and gives us a fresh start. Each morning we wake up and each breath we take is truly a gift from God. It is another opportunity to repent and to get it right with God. The Bible tells us in 1 Corinthians 15:52, "In a moment, in the twinkling of an eye, at the last trump: for the trumpet shall sound, and the dead shall be raise incorruptible, and we shall be changed." The scripture tells us when we die, whether we are right or wrong, believers or unbelievers, saved or unsaved, godly or ungodly, we will all rise again when the last trumpet sounds. The Bible tells us there will be a change; a transformation will take place immediately.

Whatever work our hands produced in this life, we will be held accountable when we stand before God.

Romans 14:12 — So then every one of us shall give account of himself to God.

Matthew 12:36-37 — But I say unto you, that every idle word that men shall speak, they shall give account thereof in the day of judgment. For by thy, words thou shalt be justified, and by thy words thou shalt be condemned.

The Robe of Sins

Hebrews 9:27 — And as it is appointed unto men once to die, but after this the judgment.

There is no scripture that tells us that there is repentance beyond the grave; there is no conversion after the last breath is drawn. This is the reason the Bible tells us in 2 Corinthians 6:2, "I tell you, now is the time of God's favor, now is the day of salvation." At some point in time, we all will have a physical death, but Christ died on the cross so that we will not have a spiritual death. Jesus came to make it possible for us to be saved. He took our place on the cross. He endured all our sins! He took pain, suffering, and judgment from us. The time to repent of all your sins is now while you still have breath in your body. Now is the time to believe in Christ, and to have a chance of eternal life.

Each of these words on "The Robe Of Sins" are consider sins and they can take on a demonic spirit... For example, there is the spirit of confusion and the spirit of manipulation. We as Christians need to be more alert and observant of how we treat one another, and what words we use when we are communicating with one another. We need to be more aware of what words we allow into our spirits. Sometimes we can allow certain words into our spirits unknowingly. They can come in by way of the company we keep, through friends and families, the music or radio shows we choose to listen to, the programs we watch on television, newspaper, catalogs, magazines, VCR's, CDs, MP3, Laptops, Billboards, e-mails, books, sporting events, plays, concerts, movies, family gathering, and all the social media we're bombarded with.

We must not forget that Satan will do anything to keep our minds off God. Satan has a way to keep us so busy, and over-stimulate our minds with so much garbage that we miss from hearing that still small voice from God. He tries to get us concerned about the flesh. Yes, he wants us to please that flesh. He wants us to keep worrying about our appearances (are we pretty enough?), getting our body parts injected with concrete and other unknown substance and then having to deal with the side effects of those injections — such as silicones bursting and leaking in the body, thereby causing other diseases to develop;

The Robe of Sins

imputation of the body parts, constantly in pain; stopping and starting different diets after making us think that we're too fat, too thin, and so we need to eat less or eat more. All of these are just Satan's attempt in wasting our time on as many good causes as possible. And those are just off the top of my head, but I'm sure there's more!

In addition, Satan has made a mockery of God-instituted marriage. Satan has got people marrying same sex, adults marrying small children; and some are even marrying their pets, laptops or computer! This is just straight up stupidity, yet society is saying, "It's okay; God still loves us." And you know what? This is true, God still loves us. Nevertheless, He also wants us to line up with His word and walk accordingly. People, please wake up! Get in a hurry about God's business. There is so much going on in this world. And it's all deterrence!

Satan studies us and he knows what traps to set for us. He waits us out for that perfect moment to throw that wrench into our lives. He uses the negative words we speak against ourselves as his tool to fight us. This is warfare. This is where he sets up strongholds in our mind. Satan is using all of these situations and conditions as weapons against us. More so, Satan has figured that as long as we're busy with the cares of this life, we'll have less time to hear as well as spend with Jesus Christ our Heavenly Father. This can also keep us from forming an intimate relationship with God. As long as we don't have that intimate relationship with God, Satan will always have the upper hand.

God's words clearly tell us not to be conformed to this world, "And be not conformed to this world: but be ye transformed by the renewing of your mind, that ye may prove what is that good, and acceptable, and perfect, will of God (Romans 12:2)." Things like this can easily happen, and whenever we fail to read our Bible, we are starving our spirit man and choosing to die a slow and painful death, spiritually and eventually physically. We need to stop speaking negative situations into existence and start speaking positive situations into existence. Satan hears every negative word that comes out of our mouth and he acts on them. Satan knows that once we have that connection with Jesus, he has no stronghold or power over us. Satan will have us thinking that we are working in our own strength. That's just another lie from Satan.

God gave us the perfect ammunition to use against Satan, which is the Holy Bible. And YES, we can use God's word as our weapon. We can do that by studying His word, through Bible studies, Christian-themed books, sermon tapes, CD's, Christian movies, preaching, teachings, schools, Christian skits, plays, concerts, seminars, and Christians TV Programs. We also should be fasting, praying, and allowing God's Holy Spirit to teach us all things about His words (weapon).

According to John 14:26, Scripture says, "But the Comforter, which is the Holy Ghost, who the Father will send in my name, He shall teach you all things, and bring all things to your remembrance, whatsoever I have said unto you. Another weapon we can use is praise. Psalm 149:6 says, "Let the high praises of God be in their mouth, and a two-edged sword in their hand." 2 Chronicles 20:22 also states, "And when they began to sing and praise, the Lord set ambushments against the children of Ammon, Moab, and mount Seir, which were come against Judah; and they were smitten."

James tells us about being obedience to God's word — "Knowing the truth about God, being obedience to God's holy word as well as being hearer and doer of God's word, can set us on the right track to eternal life (James 4:7)."

We are too often ready to compromise with the world so that we can quickly get back into our norm, our comfort zone, our feel-good mode, that we are not even aware of the type of spirits attached to these words and action that seems to find their way into our lives. At any given moment, these spirits linger around us and are ready for any opportunity to present themselves in the most harmful, hurtful, and treacherous ways. There are several ways Satan uses these words to attack us. Mostly, it is used through the people who are the closest to us, and such people include our family, friends, and church folks. Satan also gives us that false sense of security about the use of these words, by making us think that if our favorite person, family member, movie star, singer, rapper and everyone else is using these words and if society doesn't look down or frown upon it, in fact, they are joining in, then it must be okay (Romans 12:2). This way of thinking is setting ourselves up for failure and only hurting ourselves. God's words tell us that we will be held accountable on the Judgment Day.

According to Webster Dictionary, accountability means to be held accountable, answerable or to be held responsible for what a person has been given, our actions, what we did or didn't do. Paul tells us in Romans 14:12, "So then every one of us shall give account of himself to God." Romans 14:10, "But why dost thou judge thy brother? or why dost thou set at naught thy brother? for we shall all stand before the judgment seat of Christ."

These words that are listed on "The Robe of Sins" seem to be used rampantly here on earth. I seriously doubt that these words will be used in Heaven. If we are Christians and we say that we are following Jesus Christ's example, then we truly need to better hold ourselves accountable for what we do and say, and for how we treat one another. In church or out of church, as a

Christian, you should be regulating and evaluating yourself daily. And you can do that by living and walking in the Spirit of God, by spending time with God every day in meditating on His words; speaking His words; and living His words by loving your neighbor as yourself. Treat others as you would want to be treated. But, above all, we must love one another because God is LOVE. We have to remember who we are in Christ and who we are in this world. Are we checking ourselves and being about our Father's business? We as Christians have to remember what God's word tells us in John 17:16, "They are not of the world, even as I am not of the world."

God's word also tells us in Matthew 16:19 (NLT), "And I will give you the keys of the Kingdom of Heaven. Whatever you forbid on earth will be forbidden in Heaven, and whatever you permit on earth will be permitted in Heaven."

CHAPTER 2

Types of Sins

We live in a society today where many will argue over what's right and what's wrong and what is considered a sin and what is not a sin. When we think of sin, we immediately think of the violation of the Ten Commandments. Some of the first sins that come to mind are lying, adultery, idolatry, hate, and disobedience. But, my question is, "Are these words really sins?" or "Do we give life to these sinful words whenever we act upon them?" or "Are these words considered sinful when they stand alone?" or "Do they become sinful words when we give birth to them by acting upon them and implementing them into our daily lives?" Therefore, by giving them life, this could ultimately take your life!

The New Living Translation commentary gives an excellent example using the word temptation below:

"Why does Satan tempt us? Temptation is Satan's invitation to give in to his kind of life and give up on God's kind of life. Satan tempted Eve and succeeded in getting her to sin. Ever since then, he's been busy getting people to sin. He even tempted Jesus (Matthew 4:1-11). But Jesus did not sin! How could Eve have resisted temptation?

First, we must realize that being tempted is not a sin. We have not sinned until we give in to the temptation. Then, to resist temptation, we must (1) pray for strength to resist, (2) run, sometimes literally, and (3) say no when confronted with what we know is wrong. James 1:12 tells of the blessings and rewards for those who don't give in when tempted."

The Robe of Sins

"Blessed is the man that endureth temptation: for when he shall receive the crown of life, which the Lord hath promised to them that love him (James 1:12)."

James 1:13-15 tells of the destruction and death when we give in to temptation:

"Let no man say when he is tempted, I am tempted of God: for God cannot be tempted with evil, neither tempted he any man: But every man is tempted, when he is drawn away of his own lust, and enticed. Then when lust hath conceived, it bringeth forth sin: and sin, when it is finished, bringeth forth death (James 1:13-15)."

Let's look at the word poverty. People living in poverty do not have enough money for basic necessities such as food and shelter. Poverty is the state of being poor, having little money or being in need of a specific quality. An example of poverty is the state wherein a person is homeless and has no money or assets. One may ask the question, "Is poverty a sin? Yes, poverty is a sin. However, if you live in poverty, that do not make you a sinner. But when you accept poverty as a normality in your life, then that is when poverty becomes a sin. Poverty causes good people to do bad things. In other words, there are a lot of negative things that are birthed out of this word poverty. For example, poverty can engender undue desperation when we can't meet our bills; get a job, shelter, and clothes; feed our families; and obtain health insurance, life insurance and dental insurance. We may go overboard when we cannot cover the very basic needs of our families.

When people's back is against the wall and they feel that they can't cope with the situation, most of the time, they turn to a life of crime. That is when you begin to see the actions of those other words pop up—like steal, kill, murder, destroy, lying, jealousy, alcoholic, hate, backbiting, deceit, whoremongers, prostitution, drug addiction, etc. All of these sins are usually committed by individuals in order to survive their state of living in poverty.

Please understand that I'm not saying that it's okay to do these things, and I'm also not saying

The Robe of Sins

that poverty is an excuse to do these things. But, what I am saying is that MOST of the time, it is out of poverty that these things are birthed. Is it right to do these awful things? Absolutely not! However, when you have that intimate relationship with Christ, He is your way out of poverty.

Poverty also means an extremely poor person. And the Bible clearly tells us in Mark 14:7 "that the poor will be with us always."'

Let's look at another word Anger. Was Jesus ever angry? Yes, Jesus showed anger on more than one occasion. Is the word anger a sin? Anger itself is not wrong. It depends on what makes us angry and what we do with our anger. Too often, we express our anger in selfish and harmful ways. By contrast, Jesus expressed His anger by correcting a problem—healing a man's withered hand. We can use our anger to finding good solutions to help build people up rather than to tear people down. We love God and we know that God is love. And we know that surely, God cannot see Himself in our anger. God has to be able to see Himself in us. We are of reflection of Him. The moment God can't see Himself in us, then our kingdom will begin to fall.

To reign over the rest of the world that God gave us dominion over, first we must be ready, willing and able to carry out God's command without anger. If it be that we have a calling on our lives be not afraid but be willing to put away our anger and speak the truth, be a minister of the gospel as God will have us to do so. Sometimes, in order to do God's work, we will have to make hard and tough choices. Especially when things or people begin to become a hinderance to us.

We may not always like our choices, but they have to be made. We should not speak things that are not in alignment with our assignment and we should not allow others to do so either. We must learn that with some people you just have to let go even family! But, I encourage you to do so with much prayer. Always remember we should never allow anyone to hinder our relationship with God! Matt 10:32-40 - Speaks of Jesus Christ being acknowledge in the present of others and it also speaks of the hard choices we will

The Robe of Sins

have to eventually make concerning Christ and our love ones.

Be immersed in prayer and get grounded in His words. Satan will launch His attacks on you. And the attacks will come from the people you least expect. His spirit will be influenced by unsuspected family, friends and church family. But, when others began to speak negativity over your life, do not become angry but also do not accept it. Denounce it down immediately in Jesus's name.

The Bible gives us examples of how the very people we love can speak against what we are trying to do or accomplish. Let's look at Jesus and Peter. Jesus began to explain to His disciples that He would soon suffer many things at the hands of the elders and be killed, and the third day be raised to life. Peter took Jesus aside and began to speak against what Jesus was telling them. Jesus knew that Peter did not understand the big picture and He also knew that Satan's spirit had entered into Peter - Matt 16:21-24. There is no doubt that Jesus loved His disciple Peter. But He still had to rebuke Peter. As you can see in this case, Jesus did not get angry with Peter but, instead He cast down what Peter was speaking, because Jesus knew what God's plan for mankind were. He knew He had to make things right again between man and His Father Jehovah God. The Bible says in Matt 16:23 NKJV – "But he turned and said to Peter, get you behind me Satan, you are an offense to me; for you mind not the thing that be of God but those that be of men."

When we are grounded in God 's word, He will give us strength to stand against Satan. He will teach us how to stand still and know that He is God. Stand still and see the salvation of the Lord.

According to WIKIPEDIA, "Righteous indignation is typically a reactive emotion of anger over mistreatment, insult, or malice...In some Christian doctrines, righteous anger is considered the only form of anger which is not sinful, e.g., when Jesus drove the money leaders out of the temple (Gospel of Matthew 21)."

Some may argue that Jesus should not get angry because He is Jesus! Well, let's just think about this for a moment. When Jesus saw that His

Father's house was being disrespected, He took action to protect it. Jesus' anger was completely justified. Because at its root was concern for God's holiness and worship. Jesus' quick and decisive action to correct this situation was necessary and understandable. Another time Jesus showed anger was in the synagogue of Capernaum. When the Pharisees refused to answer Jesus' questions, "He looked around at them in anger, deeply distressed at their stubborn hearts" (Mark 3:5 NIV). Ephesians 4:26 instructs us, "in your anger do not sin and not to let the sun go down on our anger." This does not mean that we should ignore, suppress or avoid anger, but to deal with it accordingly, properly, and in a timely manner.

A short summary of the GotQuestions.Org explains how "Jesus Christ set a good example for man on how to deal with anger. It shows how each of Jesus' display of anger showed the proper motivation and concern for the right reasons. He was focused and was not angry at God or at the weakness of others. He was upset over the Pharisees' lack of faith, though stemmed from His love for the Pharisees and concern for their spiritual condition. Jesus was in control and never allowed anger to turn into bitterness. Jesus' emotions were held in accordance with the will and the Word of God.1

James 1:19-20 (NLT) speaks of anger that erupts when our ego is bruised; "I am hurt," or "My opinions are not being heard." When injustice and sin occur, we should become angry because others are being hurt. But we should not become angry when we fail to win an argument or when we feel offended or neglected. Selfish anger never helps anybody.

Whenever we find ourselves dealing with anger, we should follow the example of Jesus Christ. The Bible tells us how to deal with anger — "Wherefore, my beloved brethren, let every man be swift to hear, slow to speak, slow to wrath: For the wrath of man worketh not the righteousness of God (James 1:19-20)." Jesus did not exhibit man's anger, but the righteous indignation of God.

One may ask the question, Are there different types of sins? That is a question that is highly debatable. Let's break this down.

INHERENT SIN

This sin is inherited from Adam and Eve, our earthly parents. When they sinned, their inner nature was transformed by their sin of rebellion and disobedience. This brought forth spiritual corruption and physical death. We sin because we are sinners. This type of sin is often referred to as Adamic nature or "the old man."

IMPUTED SIN

According to Webster Dictionary, "To impute is: To think of as belonging to someone, and therefore to cause it to belong to that person. Because Adam and Eve sinned, their sin was imputed into mankind." For example, God "sees" Adam and Eve's sins as belonging to us their seed. The sin of Adam and Eve has been passed down to all generations down line. However, God also sees that in justification, He thinks of Christ's righteousness as belonging to us as well. Regardless of our sinful nature or imputed sins, because of His Son Jesus' righteousness, God still can relate to us on this basis.

According to Webster Dictionary, "this word was also used in a financial setting (From en and logos (in the sense of account); to reckon in, i.e. Attribute—impute, put on account). The Greek word translated "imputed" means "to take something that belongs to someone and credit it to another's account." Before the Law of Moses was given, sin was not imputed to man; however, men were still sinners because of the inherited sin. After the Law was given, sins committed in violation of the Law were imputed (accounted) to men.

The scriptures tell us in Romans 5:12-14, "Wherefore, as by one-man sin entered into the world, and death by sin; and so, death passed upon all men, for that all have sinned: (For until the law sin was in the world: but sin is not imputed when there is no law. Nevertheless death reigned from Adam to Moses, even over them that had not sinned after the similitude of Adam's transgression, who is the figure of him that was to come."

The Robe of Sins

PERSONAL SIN

Each day, we exercise our freedom of choice that allows us to willfully use our words and actions in a good, evil or hurtful way to help, encourage or harm ourselves or other individuals. If your words and actions are not in agreement with God's word and they violate God's law, then you have committed a personal sin. All human beings commit personal and individual sins everyday whenever we knowingly and deliberately violate God's law. Personal Sins can be used in different ways; such as unintentional untruth, idol worshipping, greed, jealousy, stealing, murder, trespass, and fornication. However, all hope is not lost. When God's Son Jesus Christ died on the cross, He gave us the power to resist sin through the Holy Spirit that dwells within us.

Romans 8:9-11 — "But ye are not in the flesh, but in the Spirit, if so be that the Spirit of God dwell in you. Now if any man has not the Spirit of Christ, he is none of his. And if Christ be in you, the body is dead because of sin; but the Spirit is life because of righteousness. But if the Spirit of him that raised up Jesus from the dead dwell in you, he that raised up Christ from the dead shall also quicken your mortal bodies by his Spirit that dwelleth in you."

1 John 1:9 — "If we confess our sins, he is faithful and just to forgive us our sins, and to cleanse us from all unrighteousness."

CHAPTER 3

Levels of Sins

SIN GREATLY

Most socialites believe that there are no levels or degree of sins. They believe that all sins weigh the same. In their eyes, a sin is a sin. Whether you sin in your heart or give birth to sin by acting on the sin, they believe it's all the same. They feel that sin in any amount will separate us from God. There is only one part of this paragraph that I agree with, "Sin in any amount will separate us from God." I believe this to be true! However, the Bible tells us that some sins are worse than others, because scriptures support this theory. For example, in Genesis 13:13;18:20, God had a conversation with Abraham about the people of Sodom and Gomorrah being "extremely evil" and "excessively wicked" and were sinning greatly against God.

The Bible tells us to be aware of serious sins! In 1 Corinthians 6:9-11 (NKJV), the Bible teaches us about the unrighteousness — Do you not know that the unrighteous will not inherit the kingdom of God? Do not be deceived. Neither fornicators, nor idolaters, nor adulterers, nor homosexuals, [a] nor sodomites, nor thieves, nor covetous, nor drunkards, nor revilers, nor extortioners will inherit the kingdom of God. And such were some of you. But you were washed, but you were sanctified, but you were justified in the name of the Lord Jesus and by the Spirit of our God.

Proverbs 12:18 — There is that speaketh like the piercings of a sword: but the tongue of the wise is health.

Ephesians 4:31-32 — Let all bitterness, and wrath, and anger, and clamour, and evil speaking, be put away from you, with all malice: And be ye kind one to another, tenderhearted, forgiving one another, even as God for Christ's sake hath forgiven you.

Matthew 5:27-28 — Ye have heard that it was said by them of old time, thou shalt not commit adultery: But I say unto you, That whosoever looketh on a woman to lust after her hath committed adultery with her already in his heart.

Revelation 21:8 —But the fearful, and unbelieving, and the abominable, and murderers, and whoremongers, and sorcerers, and idolaters, and all liars, shall have their part in the lake which burneth with fire and brimstone: which is the second death.

SIN OUT OF IGNORANCE

According to WIKIPEDIA Encyclopedia, "ignorance is a lack of knowledge. The word ignorant is an adjective that describes a person in the state of being unaware and can describe individuals who do not deliberately ignore or disregard important information or facts, or individuals who are unaware of important information or facts. Ignorance can come in three different types: factual ignorance (absence of knowledge of some fact), objectual ignorance (unacquaintance with some object), and technical ignorance (absence of knowledge of how to do something)."

Some sins are committed out of ignorance and do not line up with God. It is our responsibility to read, study, and meditate on God's word so that we will not be ignorant of His Word. Why? It is foolish thinking for us to continue to sin and try to hide it from God. We can hide nothing from God. He knows all and everything we do. There are scriptures throughout the Bible that speak of ignorance.

1 Timothy 1:13 — Who was before a blasphemer, and a persecutor, and injurious: but I obtained mercy, because I did it ignorantly in unbelief.

Acts 17:30 — And the times of this ignorance God winked at; but now commandeth all men everywhere to repent.

Numbers 15:30-31 — But the soul that doeth ought presumptuously, whether he be born in the land, or a stranger, the same reproacheth the Lord; and that soul shall be cut off from among his people. Because he hath despised the word of the Lord, and hath broken his commandment, that soul shall utterly be cut off; his iniquity shall be upon him.

Jeremiah 16:17 — For mine eyes are upon all their ways: they are not hid from my face, neither is their iniquity hid from mine eyes.

Psalm 90:8 — Thou hast set our iniquities before thee, our secret sins in the light of thy countenance.

Jeremiah 23:24 — Can any hide himself in secret places that I shall not see him? saith the Lord. Do not I fill heaven and earth? saith the Lord.

Jeremiah 32:19 — Great in counsel, and mighty in work: for thine eyes are open upon all the ways of the sons of men: to give every one according to his ways, and according to the fruit of his doings.

Luke 12:2 — For there is nothing covered, that shall not be revealed; neither hid, that shall not be known.

REOCCURRENCE SINS

Some sins can become a common occurrence, for example, a high level of habitual sins happening often within a certain amount of time period. The Bible shows a difference in habitual sin and single sin. Once we know what is right and still practice sin willfully, then we deserve to receive God's adverse judgment. The Bible clearly tells us not to let man deceive us. If we are doing righteousness, then we are righteous. If we are committing sin, then we are of the devil.

1 John 3:4-8 — Whosoever committeth sin transgresseth also the law: for sin is the transgression of the law. And ye know that he was manifested to take away our sins; and in him is no sin. Whosoever abideth in him sinneth not: whosoever sinneth hath not seen him, neither known him. Little children let no man deceive you: he that doeth righteousness is righteous, even as he is righteous. He that committeth sin is of the devil; for the devil sinneth from the beginning. For this purpose, the Son of God was manifested, that he might destroy the works of the devil.

Hebrews 10:26-27 — For if we sin willfully after that we have received the knowledge of the truth, there remaineth no more sacrifice for sins, But a certain fearful looking for of judgment and fiery indignation, which shall devour the adversaries."

According to a commentary in the New Living Translation (NLT), There are a different between committing a sin and continuing to sin. Even the most faithful believers sometimes commit sins, but they do not cherish a particular sin and choose to commit it. A believer who commits a sin repents, confesses, and finds forgiveness. A person who continues to sin, by contrast, is not sorry for what he or she is doing. Thus, this person never confesses and never receives forgiveness. Such a person is in opposition to God, no matter what religious claims he or she makes.

Under the Old Testament sacrifice system, a lamb without blemish was offered as sacrifice for sin. Jesus is 'the Lamb of God who takes away sin of the world' (John 1:29). Because Jesus lived a perfect life and sacrificed himself for our sins, we can be completely forgiven. We can look back to his death for us and know that we need never suffer eternal death (1 Peter 1:18-20).[2]

"We all have areas where temptation is strong, and habits are hard to conquer. These weaknesses give the Devil a foothold, so we must deal with our areas of vulnerability. If we are struggling with a particular sin, however, these verses are not directed at us, even if for the time we seem to keep on sinning. John is not talking about people whose victories are still incomplete; he is talking about people who make a practice of sinning and look for a way to justify it."

The New Living Translation (NLT) commentary gives three steps necessary to find victory over what is called prevailing sin. John Angell James (Evidences & Results of Sanctified Affliction), explains that "The love of the world is the great snare of the church in every age! Worldly-mindedness is now the prevailing sin of Christians. We see them on all hands too eager to make themselves happy on earth, and seeking their enjoyments, if not in the sinful amusements of the world—yet in its 'innocent and home-bred comforts'. They look not at unseen and eternal things, but at seen and temporal things. Theirs is too much a life of 'sense', refined it is true from its gross sinfulness—but still a life of sense, rather than a life of faith."

The three steps are as follows:

(1) Seek the power of the Holy Spirit and God's Word.
(2) Stay away from tempting situations; and
(3) Seek the help of the body of Christ—Be open to their willingness to hold you accountable and to pray for you.

Some socialites believe that they can keep sinning. But, true Christians, true believers do not make a practice of sinning, nor do they become unsympathetic to God's moral law. Surely, they know the devastating consequences that follow sinning. All believers will still sin, and I know that God sees our daily struggles. But, I also believe that as long as we continue to stay in the fight and not give up, God will give us victory over sin.

The Bible tells us not to minimize any sins because it can cause us to violate God's Laws. The Bible also tells us that King David was one of the greatest men in the Old Testament. We think of

The Robe of Sins

him as King, Giant-Killer, Shepherd, Poet and Ancestor of Jesus. However, there was another side to King David too. King David was guilty of committing serious sins. He was an adulterer — he committed adultery with Bathsheba; a murderer — he arranged the murder of Uriah, Bathsheba's husband; a liar — he lied in order to cover up his sins; a disobedient person — he directly disobeyed God in taking a census of the people; a betrayer — he betrayed God, his Marriage vows, and his Soldier Uriah. Well, whenever King David sinned, he was quick to confess his sins, from the heart, and God knew his repentance was genuine. He never took God's forgiveness for granted and he appreciated His many blessings.

God loved King David. He referred to King David as "a man after his own heart." King David experienced the joy of forgiveness from God, yet he was still held accountable and had to suffer the consequences of his sins. I'm sure King David felt overwhelmed and weighed down. King David wrote, "My errors loom over my head; like a heavy burden they are too much for me to bear" (Psalm 38:4 NLT).

The Bible also tells us that King David might have sinned greatly, but he did not sin repeatedly; he learned from his mistakes and he learned to accept the suffering they brought.

Isaiah 55:7 — Let the wicked forsake his way, and the unrighteous man his thoughts: and let him return unto the Lord, and he will have mercy upon him; and to our God, for he will abundantly pardon.

CHAPTER 4

Who Committed the First Sin?

In order to start our fight on the battlefield against sin, first, we must get an understanding of how sin began. We must understand that our mind is where we process everything. Therefore, it is very important to have control over what we allow into our mind. You see, there is a spiritual war going on, and our mind is the battlefield; meaning that there is a war going on between your spirit man and your flesh man. They are always fighting each other about doing what is right versus what is wrong. However, in the beginning, things did not start out that way. Based on my studies of the Bible, those three words PRIDE, JEALOUSY and DISOBEDIENCE played a major part in how things unfolded in heaven and here on earth. According to Isaiah 14:12-15, it was Lucifer, later renamed Satan, who committed the first sin. Satan was the most powerful, beautiful angel of all the angels. He wanted to be like God and he was jealous of God, and that became the beginning of sin and Satan's downfall.

"How art thou fallen from heaven, O Lucifer, son of the morning! How art thou cut down to the ground, which didst weaken the nations! For thou hast said in thine heart, I will ascend into heaven, I will exalt my throne above the stars of God: I will sit also upon the mount of the congregation, in the sides of the north: I will ascend above the height of the clouds: I will be like the most High. Yet thou shalt be brought down to hell, to the sides of the pit. "

The Robe of Sins

Once Satan was kicked out of heaven and roaming around earth, it was then he introduced sin to Eve and Adam when they were in the Garden. He tempted them with the very same enticement, "You shall be like God, knowing the good and the evil."

Have you ever thought about what things would be like for us if Adam and Eve had never eaten from the forbidding tree? We would possibly be living a perfect life in the Garden of Eden the way God had intended it to be; living in paradise here on earth, with no death, pain, sorrow or evilness. Well, before the first sin was committed, that is exactly how God wanted mankind to live—to be fruitful and multiply. After God created Adam and Eve, He instructed Adam not to eat from the forbidden tree.

Genesis 2:15-25 explains the relationship between God, Adam and Eve; and at the beginning, it was good. "And the Lord God took the man and put him into the garden of Eden to dress it and to keep it. And the Lord God commanded the man, saying, Of every tree of the garden thou mayest freely eat: But of the tree of the knowledge of good and evil, thou shalt not eat of it: for in the day that thou eatest thereof thou shalt surely die. And Adam gave names to all cattle, and to the fowl of the air, and to every beast of the field; but for Adam there was not found a help meet for him. And the Lord God caused a deep sleep to fall upon Adam, and he slept: and he took one of his ribs and closed up the flesh instead thereof; And the rib, which the Lord God had taken from man, made he a woman, and brought her unto the man. And Adam said, This is now bone of my bones, and flesh of my flesh: she shall be called Woman, because she was taken out of Man. And they were both naked, the man and his wife, and were not ashamed."

Genesis 1:28 says, "And God blessed them, and God said unto them, Be fruitful, and multiply, and replenish the earth, and subdue it: and have dominion over the fish of the sea, and over the fowl of the air, and over every living thing that moveth upon the earth."

Genesis 3 tells us how Adam and Eve turned on God and believed Satan's word over God's. We have inherited sin from our first earthly parents,

The Robe of Sins

our ancestors Adam and Eve. Sin was carried out through all the generations of mankind.

Genesis 3:1-8 — Now the serpent was more subtle than any beast of the field which the Lord God had made. And he said unto the woman, Yea, hath God said, Ye shall not eat of every tree of the garden? And the woman said unto the serpent, We may eat of the fruit of the trees of the garden: But of the fruit of the tree which is in the midst of the garden, God hath said, Ye shall not eat of it, neither shall ye touch it, lest ye die. And the serpent said unto the woman, Ye shall not surely die: For God doth know that in the day ye eat thereof, then your eyes shall be opened, and ye shall be as gods, knowing good and evil. And when the woman saw that the tree was good for food, and that it was pleasant to the eyes, and a tree to be desired to make one wise, she took of the fruit thereof, and did eat, and gave also unto her husband with her; and he did eat. And the eyes of them both were opened, and they knew that they were naked; and they sewed fig leaves together and made themselves aprons. And they heard the voice of the Lord God walking in the garden in the cool of the day: and Adam and his wife hid themselves from the presence of the Lord God amongst the trees of the garden.

The Bible tells us Adam and Eve hid themselves behind fig-leaf aprons and later behind the trees. Like Adam and Eve, when we are not doing the right thing, we try to hide ourselves (our sins) from the "presence of the Lord." (Genesis 3:8). But, what we fail to realize is that when we try to hide our sins, God will seek us out, just like He did our parents—Adam and Eve. As God walked in the garden, He asked the question, "Where are you?" (Genesis 3:9).

That is a very good question! We might want to ask ourselves that same question. Where are YOU in Christ? If the sky cracks open and Jesus comes back for His Church, His bride, where will you be found—in Him or sin? Will YOU be READY? Right now, this very minute? If YOUR answer is NO, then YOU need to get ready and, in a hurry, because we are truly living in the last days. Scriptures don't LIE. As you read 2 Timothy 3:1-17, you will notice some of those very words listed on "The Robe Of Sins"

The Robe of Sins

are listed in this scripture passage, which reveals that in "the last days, perilous times shall come."

The Bible tells us that the Lord came looking for Adam and Eve to have a conversation with them. But, because they were disobedient by eating from the forbidden tree, they broke the spiritual rim between God and them. That was when the first spiritual death took place in the garden. Adam and Eve felt the spiritual separation that took place between God and them. They had to have felt the change in the atmosphere of the relationship. However, the physical death did not come until much later. God told them that they would return to the ground. In other word, they would eventually die (Genesis 3:19).

One can only imagine when Adam heard God call out to him in the Garden, that he really did not want to answer. He knew he had some explaining to do because he had sinned. Adam did not want to have that conversation! Adam and Eve were naked and afraid, not knowing what punishment they were about to face. Adam knew what God had told him concerning the forbidden tree. For the first time, death, fear, shame, blame, and disobedience were present (Genesis 2:16-17).

Genesis 3:9-12 — And the Lord God called unto Adam, and said unto him, Where art thou? And he said, I heard thy voice in the garden, and I was afraid, because I was naked; and I hid myself. And he said, Who told thee that thou was naked? Hast thou eaten of the tree, whereof I commanded thee that thou shouldest not eat? And the man said, The woman whom thou gavest to be with me, she gave me of the tree, and I did eat. (KJV)

Satan had Adam and Eve so confused that at some point, they began to blame God, each other, and Satan for their downfall. Adam began to blame God by pointing out to God that "it was that WOMAN that YOU gave me, SHE told me to eat and I did it." And the woman blamed the serpent. Genesis 3:13 says, "And the Lord God said unto the woman, what is this that thou hast done? And the woman said, the SERPENT beguiled me, and I did eat."

If you think about it, you will see there is nothing new under the sun. Many generations later, and here, we are today doing the very same thing, playing the blame game—blaming God, others, and Satan for our sins. God gave us choices, that is, "free will" to sin or not to sin. And, we clearly know what God's word says about sins. Let's be real with ourselves, Satan is not to blame for everything that goes wrong in our individual life. Yes, he is on his job; and we need to be about God's business too. Time and time again, Satan continues to come to us with the same old tricks. Satan comes to launch his attacks, by way of the flesh, disease, poverty, jealousy, sickness, and all those other words listed on "The Robe Of Sins."

Also, whenever we use negative words, Satan uses those very words as weapon against us. It starts eating us up from the inside out, thus affecting our mind, thoughts, and attitude. It also manifests into our action on how we treat one another. Those very words that proceed out of our mouth give Satan ammunition and weapons he needs to kill our spirit and the spirit of our families, friends, neighbors, churches, and our communities.

Many of us say that we are of God and that we are living by God's example; yet we are murdering one another at a rapid rate, both physically and verbally with our hateful heart and words on a daily basis. Each time we spew those negative words out of our mouths, we become the supplier of ammunition to Satan who then uses that against us or our neighbors or our relatives. Don't you know until Jesus Christ returns, Satan will always have a steady ready supply of weapons of destructions to use against you? Get in the word of God, realize and get the understanding that this is a spiritual war that starts in the mind, and the mind is the battlefield. We must know that God needs more soldiers on the battlefield to help combat Satan. And we can do this by studying our Bible and forming that inmate relationship with God. The word of God is our weapon.

You should always be on alert and realize that this is Satan's world for now. Remember that old saying "an idle hand is Satan's workshop." I believe this to be true. So, in this case, your mind must be alert, lest it becomes the stronghold of

Satan. Satan is a major influence over people, their mind, goals, opinions, ideas, and their thoughts. Ephesians 2:2 says that Satan is the prince of the power of the air — "Wherein in time past ye walked according to the course of this world, according to the prince of the power of the air, the spirit that now worketh in children of disobedience." Satan is called prince because he is a ruler and has the power to manifest evil influence through people and his demons (Revelation 2:13). When God asked Satan where he has been, he said he was going up and down the earth. Job 1:6-7 (GNT) — "When the day came for the heavenly beings to appear before the Lord, Satan was there among them. The Lord asked him, 'What have you been doing?' Satan answered, 'I have been walking here and there, roaming around the earth.'" So, as you can see, Satan is always on his job looking to see who he can devour. And we can be on our job as well by staying in God's word, being obedient.

God's word tells us in Romans 6:23 that "the wages of sin is death, but the gift of God is eternal life in Christ Jesus our Lord." Romans 5 :12

(NIV) also says, "Therefore, just as sin entered the world through one man, and death through sin, and in this way, death came to all people, because all sinned."

CHAPTER 5

Punishment for Sin and Disobeying God

Even though God loved Adam and Eve, He became upset with them and passed out their punishment for disobeying Him. God also handed down Satan's punishment as well.

First, God gave out the Serpent's (Satan) Punishment.

Genesis 3:14-15 — And the Lord God said unto the serpent, Because thou hast done this, thou art cursed above all cattle, and above every beast of the field; upon thy belly shalt thou go, and dust shalt thou eat all the days of thy life: And I will put enmity between thee and the woman, and between thy seed and her seed; it shall bruise thy head, and thou shalt bruise his heel.

Second, God gave out the Woman's Punishment.

Genesis 3:16 — Unto the woman he said, I will greatly multiply thy sorrow and thy conception; in sorrow thou shalt bring forth children; and thy desire shall be to thy husband, and he shall rule over thee.

And third, God gave Adam's Punishment as well as all generations that follow.

Genesis 3:17-19 — And unto Adam he said, Because thou hast hearkened unto the voice of thy wife, and hast eaten of the tree, of which I commanded thee, saying, Thou shalt not eat of it: cursed is the ground for thy sake; in sorrow shalt thou eat of it all the days of thy life; Thorns also and thistles shall it bring forth to thee; and thou shalt eat the herb of the field; In the sweat of thy face shalt thou eat bread, till thou return unto the ground; for out of it wast thou taken: for dust thou art, and unto dust shalt thou return.

CHAPTER 6

The First Sacrifice to Cover the First Sin

After Adam and Eve sinned, their eyes were opened, and they realized they were naked. They made clothes for themselves by sewing fig leaves

The Robe of Sins

together. See Genesis 3:7. However, after God came into the Garden and saw them hiding and wearing fig leaves, He was not pleased. Why were the fig leaves not good enough to cover God's greatest creation? Let's look a little closer.

After declaring Adam and Eve's punishment for disobeying Him, God did cover them again, but not with the glory of God. He covered them with animal skin. The Bible tells us in Genesis 3:21 that "unto Adam also and his wife did the Lord God make coats of skins and clothed them."

This act caused God to commit the very first killing, sacrifice in the Bible. God killed two of the animals to get their skin to cover Adam and Eve's nakedness—by implication, their sin. From the beginning, God has declared that the recompense for sin is death, and so blood must be shed to cover sin. The innocent dies for the guilty. This was the first shedding of innocent blood, to protect the two guilty people. Their sins' remission came at the price of the death of two innocent (blameless) animals.

Leviticus 17:11 — For the life of the flesh is in the blood: and I have given it to you upon the altar to make an atonement for yourselves on the altar: for it is the blood that makes atonement for one's life.

Hebrews 9:22 — And almost all things are by the law purged with blood; and without shedding of blood is no remission (forgiveness).

Likewise, our Lord and Savior Jesus Christ died for our inherited sin from Adam and Eve. In 1 Peter 3:18 (NKJV), the Bible tells us, "For Christ also suffered once for sins, the just for the unjust, that He might bring us to God, being put to death in the flesh... Christ also suffered when He died for our sin once for all time. He never sinned but died for sinners that he might bring us safely home to God. He suffered physical death, but he was raised to life in the spirit (NLT)."

Ephesians 2:18 — For through him we both have access by one spirit unto the Father.

The Robe of Sins

1 John 2:2 — And he is the propitiation for our sins: and not for our only, but also for the sins of the whole world.

Hebrews 9:26-28 — If that had been necessary, he would had to die again and again ever since the world began. But NO! He come once for all time, at the end of the age, to remove the power of sin forever by his sacrificial death for us. And just as it is destined that each person dies only once that after that comes judgment. So also, Christ died only once as a sacrifice to take away the sin of many people. He will come again but not to deal with our sins again. This time he will bring salvation to all those who are eagerly waiting for him (NLT).

CHAPTER 7

How Sin Affects our Relationship with God

After Adam and Eve had their experience in the Garden and disobeyed God, they no longer deserved paradise, and God told them to leave (Genesis 3:22). According to the Bible, Genesis 3:22-24 reveals that "if they had continued to live in the garden and eat from the tree of life, they would have lived forever. But eternal life in a state of sin would mean forever trying to hide from God (NLT)." Like Adam and Eve, all of us have sinned and are separated from fellowship with God. We do not have to stay separated, however. God is preparing a new earth as an eternal paradise for His people (Revelation 21-22).

Because Adam and Eve are our first parents, we have a human nature to sin. One might say it's in us, being our physical characteristics; it's our DNA from our first parents. King David spoke of this human nature in Psalm 51:5 (NIV), saying, "Surely I was sinful at birth, sinful from the time my mother conceived me."

Anytime we sin, it changes the atmosphere, strains our relationship and pushes us farther away from God. This type of behavior puts us directly on the path of hell. Our sin also hurts God's heart because He loves us and wants all of us to make it into heaven. The Bible tells us in Isaiah 59:1-2, "Behold, the LORD'S hand is not shortened, that it cannot save; neither his ear heavy, that it cannot hear; But your iniquities have separated between you and your God, and your sins have hid his face from you, that he will not hear." According to the letter of the Apostle Paul, Romans 3:23 tells us, "All have sinned and fall short of the glory of God;" and Romans 3:20 (NIV) says, "Therefore no one will be declared righteous in His sight by observing the law; rather; through the law we become conscious of sin."

1 John 1:8-10 — "If we say that we have no sin, we deceive ourselves, and the truth is not in us. If we confess our sins, He is faithful and just to forgive us our sins, and to cleanse us from all unrighteousness. If we say that we have not sinned, we make Him a liar, and His word is not in us."

After all these events took place in the Garden of Eden with Adam and Eve disobeying God, He still gave us a way out. He made provision for our salvation from sin. John 3:16-21 states, "For God so loved the world, that he gave his only begotten Son, that whosoever believeth in him should not perish, but have everlasting life. For God sent not his Son into the world to condemn the world; but that the world through him might be saved. He that believeth on him is not condemned: but he that believeth not is condemned already, because he hath not believed in the name of the only begotten Son of God. And this is the condemnation, that light is come into the world, and men loved darkness rather than light, because their deeds were evil. For everyone that doeth evil hateth the light, neither cometh to the light, lest his deeds should be reproved. But he that doeth truth cometh to the light, that his deeds may be made manifest, that they are wrought in God" (KJV).

The Bible offers different terms to better help us understand the spiritual side of each word depicted on "The Robe Of Sins." As you study, you will discover that each word brings its own pain, hardship, suffering, and difficulties. I am in absolute awe of how Jesus Christ my Lord and Savior took all of the sins of the world upon His shoulder so that we may have eternal life.

As God shared with me in an open vision of the words displayed on "The Robe Of Sins," each word is individual and is used spiritually in the Bible. I pray that you gain knowledge and a better understanding of what it really means when you hear, envision, or think of Jesus taking up all of our sins and carrying them upon His shoulder to the cross...or putting them on just like a robe, so that we may have everlasting life. Yes, no doubt, there are many other words that could easily have made the list; however, those shared in this book are the words I saw on The Robe Of Sins.

CHAPTER 8

The Robe of Sins Word Listing and Scriptures

ABOMINABLE

Proverbs 17:15 - He that justifieth the wicked, and he that condemneth the just, even they both [are] abomination to the LORD.

Proverbs 15:8 - The sacrifice of the wicked [is] an abomination to the LORD: but the prayer of the upright [is] his delight.

Proverbs 16:5 - Every one [that is] proud in heart [is] an abomination to the LORD: [though] hand [join] in hand, he shall not be unpunished.

Proverbs 28:9 - He that turneth away his ear from hearing the law, even his prayer [shall be] abomination.

Proverbs 11:20 - They that are of a froward heart [are] abomination to the LORD: but [such as are] upright in [their] way [are] his delight.

Proverbs 20:10 - Divers weights, [and] divers measures, both of them [are] alike abomination to the LORD.

Proverbs 15:26 - The thoughts of the wicked [are] an abomination to the LORD: but [the words] of the pure [are] pleasant words.

ABUSE

Ephesians 6:4 - And, ye fathers, provoke not your children to wrath: but bring them up in the nurture and admonition of the Lord.

Galatians 5:19 - Now the works of the flesh are manifest, which are [these]; Adultery, fornication, uncleanness, lasciviousness,

Proverbs 22:10 - Cast out the scorner, and contention shall go out; yea, strife and reproach shall cease.

James 5:16 - Confess [your] faults one to another, and pray one for another, that ye may be healed. The effectual fervent prayer of a righteous man availeth much.

Ecclesiastes 7:26 - And I find more bitter than death the woman, whose heart [is] snares and nets, [and] her hands [as] bands: whoso pleaseth God shall escape from her; but the sinner shall be taken by her.

ACCUSATION

1 Peter 3:16 - Having a good conscience; that, whereas they speak evil of you, as of evildoers, they may be ashamed that falsely accuse your good conversation in Christ.

Deuteronomy 19:19 - Then shall ye do unto him, as he had thought to have done unto his brother: so shalt thou put the evil away from among you.

Revelation 12:10 - And I heard a loud voice saying in heaven, Now is come salvation, and strength, and the kingdom of our God, and the power of his Christ: for the accuser of our brethren is cast down, which accused them before our God day and night.

Genesis 50:20 - But as for you, ye thought evil against me; [but] God meant it unto good, to bring to pass, as [it is] this day, to save much people alive.

Leviticus 19:16 - Thou shalt not go up and down [as] a talebearer among thy people: neither shalt thou stand against the blood of thy neighbor: I [am] the LORD.

Matthew 24:35 - Heaven and earth shall pass away, but my words shall not pass away.

ADDICTIONS

James 1:12 - Blessed [is] the man that endureth temptation: for when he is tried, he shall receive the crown of life, which the Lord hath promised to them that love him.

1 John 2:16 - For all that [is] in the world, the lust of the flesh, and the lust of the eyes, and the pride of life, is not of the Father, but is of the world.

1 Corinthians 6:12 - All things are lawful unto me, but all things are not expedient: all things are lawful for me, but I will not be brought under the power of any.

Romans 13:14 - But put ye on the Lord Jesus Christ, and make not provision for the flesh, to [fulfil] the lusts [thereof].

Galatians 5:16 - [This] I say then, Walk in the Spirit, and ye shall not fulfil the lust of the flesh.

John 8:36 - If the Son therefore shall make you free, ye shall be free indeed.

ADULTERY

Proverbs 6:32 - [But] whoso committeth adultery with a woman lacketh understanding: he [that] doeth it destroyeth his own soul.

Matthew 5:28 - But I say unto you, That whosoever looketh on a woman to lust after her hath committed adultery with her already in his heart.

Hebrews 13:4 - Marriage [is] honourable in all, and the bed undefiled: but whoremongers and adulterers God will judge.

Exodus 20:14 - Thou shalt not commit adultery.

John 8:4 - They say unto him, Master, this woman was taken in adultery, in the very act.

Matthew 5:32 - But I say unto you, That whosoever shall put away his wife, saving for the cause of fornication, causeth her to commit adultery: and whosoever shall marry her that is divorced committeth adultery.

Romans 7:3 - So then if, while [her] husband liveth, she be married to another man, she shall be called an adulteress: but if her husband be dead, she is free from that law; so that she is no adulteress, though she be married to another man.

AFFLICTION

2 Corinthians 4:16 - For which cause we faint not; but though our outward man perish, yet the inward [man] is renewed day by day.

Psalms 34:19 - Many [are] the afflictions of the righteous: but the LORD delivereth him out of them all.

Psalms 119:71 - [It is] good for me that I have been afflicted; that I might learn thy statutes.

Psalms 22:24 - For he hath not despised nor abhorred the affliction of the afflicted; neither hath he hid his face from him; but when he cried unto him, he heard.

2 Corinthians 4:17 - For our light affliction, which is but for a moment, worketh for us a far more exceeding [and] eternal weight of glory;

Job 10:15 - If I be wicked, woe unto me; and [if] I be righteous, [yet] will I not lift up my head.

[I am] full of confusion; therefore see thou mine affliction;

ANGER

Psalms 37:8 - Cease from anger, and forsake wrath: fret not thyself in any wise to do evil.

Proverbs 15:1 - A soft answer turneth away wrath: but grievous words stir up anger.

James 1:19 - Wherefore, my beloved brethren, let every man be swift to hear, slow to speak, slow to wrath:

Ecclesiastes 7:9 - Be not hasty in thy spirit to be angry: for anger resteth in the bosom of fools.

Proverbs 29:11 - A fool uttereth all his mind: but a wise [man] keepeth it in till afterwards.

Psalms 103:8 - The LORD [is] merciful and gracious, slow to anger, and plenteous in mercy.

Matthew 5:22 - But I say unto you, That whosoever is angry with his brother without a cause shall be in danger of the judgment: and whosoever shall say to his brother, Raca, shall be in danger of the council: but whosoever shall say, Thou fool, shall be in danger of hell fire.

ANGUISH

2 Samuel 1:9 - He said unto me again, Stand, I pray thee, upon me, and slay me: for anguish is come upon me, because my life is yet whole in me.

Job 7:11 - Therefore I will not refrain my mouth; I will speak in the anguish of my spirit; I will complain in the bitterness of my soul.

Psalms 41:3 - The LORD will strengthen him upon the bed of languishing: thou wilt make all his bed in his sickness.

Psalms 119:143 - Trouble and anguish have taken hold on me: yet thy commandments are my delights.

Proverbs 1:27- When your fear cometh as desolation, and your destruction cometh as a whirlwind; when distress and anguish cometh upon you.

Romans 2:9 - Tribulation and anguish upon every soul of man that doeth evil, of the Jew first, and also of the Gentile;

ANXIETY

Matthew 6:25 - Therefore I say unto you, Take no thought for your life, what ye shall eat, or what ye shall drink; nor yet for your body, what ye shall put on. Is not the life more than meat, and the body than raiment?

1 Peter 5:6 - Humble yourselves therefore under the mighty hand of God, that he may exalt you in due time:

Hebrews 13:6 - So that we may boldly say, The Lord [is] my helper, and I will not fear what man shall do unto me.

1 Peter 5:10 - But the God of all grace, who hath called us unto his eternal glory by Christ Jesus, after that ye have suffered a while, make you perfect, stablish, strengthen, settle [you].

Psalms 32:8 - I will instruct thee and teach thee in the way which thou shalt go: I will guide thee with mine eye.

John 14:27 - Peace I leave with you, my peace I give unto you: not as the world giveth, give I unto you. Let not your heart be troubled, neither let it be afraid.

John 14:1 - Let not your heart be troubled: ye believe in God, believe also in me.

Psalms 34:14 - Depart from evil, and do good; seek peace, and pursue it.

BACKSLIDER

Jeremiah 3:14 – 'Turn, O backsliding children saith the LORD; for I am married unto you: and I will take you one of a city, and two of a family, and I will bring you to Zion.

Hebrews 6:6 - If they shall fall away, to renew them again unto repentance; seeing they crucify to themselves the Son of God afresh, and put [him] to an open shame.

Proverbs 24:16 - For a just [man] falleth seven times, and riseth up again: but the wicked shall fall into mischief.

Jeremiah 8:5 - Why [then] is this people of Jerusalem slidden back by a perpetual backsliding? they hold fast deceit, they refuse to return.

Jeremiah 3:22 - Return, ye backsliding children, [and] I will heal your backslidings. Behold, we come unto thee; for thou [art] the LORD our God.

Jeremiah 14:7 - O LORD, though our iniquities testify against us, do thou [it] for thy name's sake: for our backslidings are many; we have sinned against thee.

Proverbs 14:14 - The backslider in heart shall be filled with his own ways: and a good man [shall be satisfied] from himself.

Jeremiah 24:7 - And I will give them an heart to know me, that I [am] the LORD: and they shall be my people, and I will be their God: for they shall return unto me with their whole heart.

Luke 9:62 - And Jesus said unto him, No man, having put his hand to the plough, and looking back, is fit for the kingdom of God.

Hosea 14:4 - I will heal their backsliding, I will love them freely: for mine anger is turned away from him.

BETRAY

Matthew 24:10 - And then shall many be offended, and shall betray one another, and shall hate one another.

Luke 22:48 - But Jesus said unto him, Judas, betrayest thou the Son of man with a kiss?

James 1:8 – A double minded man [is] unstable in all his ways.

Psalms 41:9 - Yea, mine own familiar friend, in whom I trusted, which did eat of my bread, hath lifted up [his] heel against me.

Luke 22:4 – And he went his way, and communed with the chief priests and captains, how he might betray him unto them.

John 13:21 - When Jesus had thus said, he was troubled in spirit, and testified, and said, Verily, verily, I say unto you, that one of you shall betray me.

BITTERNESS

Ephesians 4:31 - Let all bitterness, and wrath, and anger, and clamour, and evil speaking, be put away from you, with all malice:

Hebrews 12:15- Looking diligently lest any man fail of the grace of God; lest any root of bitterness springing up trouble [you], and thereby many be defiled.

Romans 12:18 - If it be possible, as much as lieth in you, live peaceably with all men.

Romans 12:20 - Therefore if thine enemy hunger, feed him; if he thirst, give him drink: for in so doing thou shalt heap coals of fire on his head.

Romans 12:21 - Be not overcome of evil, but overcome evil with good.

Acts 8:23 - For I perceive that thou art in the gall of bitterness, and [in] the bond of iniquity

BLASPHEMY

Matthew 12:31- Wherefore I say unto you, All manner of sin and blasphemy shall be forgiven unto men: but the blasphemy [against] the [Holy] Ghost shall not be forgiven unto men.

Matthew 12:32 - And whosoever speaketh a word against the Son of man, it shall be forgiven him: but whosoever speaketh against the Holy Ghost, it shall not be forgiven him, neither in this world, neither in the [world] to come.

Luke 12:10 - And whosoever shall speak a word against the Son of man, it shall be forgiven him: but unto him that blasphemeth against the Holy Ghost it shall not be forgiven.

Titus 2:5 - [To be] discreet, chaste, keepers at home, good, obedient to their own husbands, that the word of God be not blasphemed.

James 2:6 - But ye have despised the poor. Do not rich men oppress you, and draw you before the judgment seats?

James 2:7 - Do not they blaspheme that worthy name by the which ye are called?

Mark 3:29 - But he that shall blaspheme against the Holy Ghost hath never forgiveness, but is in danger of eternal damnation:

Revelation 13:6 - And he opened his mouth in blasphemy against God, to blaspheme his name, and his tabernacle, and them that dwell in heaven.

Revelation 13:1 - And I stood upon the sand of the sea, and saw a beast rise up out of the sea, having seven heads and ten horns, and upon his horns ten crowns, and upon his heads the name of blasphemy.

Mark 2:7 - Why doth this [man] thus speak blasphemies? who can forgive sins but God only?

BOAST

James 4:16 - But now ye rejoice in your boastings: all such rejoicing is evil.

Jeremiah 9:23 - Thus saith the LORD, Let not the wise [man] glory in his wisdom, neither let the mighty [man] glory in his might, let not the rich [man] glory in his riches:

Proverbs 27:2 - Let another man praise thee, and not thine own mouth; a stranger, and not thine own lips.

Proverbs 27:1 - Boast not thyself of tomorrow; for thou knowest not what a day may bring forth.

Ephesians 2:8 - For by grace are ye saved through faith; and that not of yourselves: [it is] the gift of God:

Psalms 94:4 - [How long] shall they utter [and] speak hard things? [and] all the workers of iniquity boast themselves?

2 Corinthians 10:12 - For we dare not make ourselves of the number, or compare ourselves with some that commend themselves: but they measuring themselves by themselves, and comparing themselves among themselves, are not wise.

2 Corinthians 10:16 - to preach the gospel in the [regions] beyond you, [and] not to boast in another man's line of things made ready to our hand.

Ephesians 2:9 - not of works, lest any man should boast.

James 3:5 - even so the tongue is a little member, and boasteth great things. Behold, how great a matter a little fire kindleth!

Proverbs 25:14 - whoso boasteth himself of a false gift [is like] clouds and wind without rain.

BONDAGE

1 John 1:9 - If we confess our sins, he is faithful and just to forgive us [our] sins, and to cleanse us from all unrighteousness.

Leviticus 26:1- Ye shall make you no idols nor graven image, neither rear you up a standing image, neither shall ye set up [any] image of stone in your land, to bow down unto it: for I [am] the LORD your God.

James 4:7 - Submit yourselves therefore to God. Resist the devil, and he will flee from you.

Genesis 4:1 - And Adam knew Eve his wife; and she conceived, and bare Cain, and said, I have gotten a man from the LORD.

2 Peter 2:19 - While they promise them liberty, they themselves are the servants of corruption: for of whom a man is overcome, of the same is he brought in bondage.

BURDEN

Matthew 11:30 - For my yoke is easy, and my burden is light.

Psalms 55:22 - Cast thy burden upon the LORD, and he shall sustain thee: he shall never suffer the righteous to be moved.

Matthew 11:28 - Come unto me, all [ye] that labour and are heavy laden, and I will give you rest.

Matthew 11:29 - Take my yoke upon you and learn from me, for I am gentle and humble in heart, and you will find rest for your souls.

Galatians 6:2 - Bear ye one another's burdens, and so fulfill the law of Christ.

CHEATER

James 4:17 - Therefore to him that knoweth to do good, and doeth [it] not, to him it is sin.

Proverbs 12:22 - Lying lips [are] abomination to the LORD: but they that deal truly [are] his delight.

Proverbs 10:9 - He that walketh uprightly walketh surely: but he that perverteth his ways shall be known.

Galatians 6:8 - For he that soweth to his flesh shall of the flesh reap corruption; but he that soweth to the Spirit shall of the Spirit reap life everlasting.

Proverbs 6:32 - [But] whoso committeth adultery with a woman lacketh understanding: he [that] doeth it destroyeth his own soul.

Proverbs 28:6 - Better [is] the poor that walketh in his uprightness, than [he that is] perverse [in his] ways, though he [be] rich.

Colossians 3:9 - Lie not one to another, seeing that ye have put off the old man with his deeds;

COMPLAINER

Philippians 2:14 - Do all things without murmurings and disputing:

Ephesians 4:29 - Let no corrupt communication proceed out of your mouth, but that which is good to the use of edifying, that it may minister grace unto the hearers.

1 Thessalonians 5:18 - In everything give thanks: for this is the will of God in Christ Jesus concerning you.

Numbers 11:1 - And [when] the people complained, it displeased the LORD: and the LORD heard [it]; and his anger was kindled; and the fire of the LORD burnt among them, and consumed [them that were] in the uttermost parts of the camp.

1 Corinthians 10:10 - Neither murmur ye, as some of them also murmured, and were destroyed of the destroyer.

Philippians 4:11 - Not that I speak in respect of want: for I have learned, in whatsoever state I am, [therewith] to be content.

Psalms 106:25 - But murmured in their tents, [and] hearkened not unto the voice of the LORD.

Isaiah 53:7 - He was oppressed, and he was afflicted, yet he opened not his mouth: he is brought as a lamb to the slaughter, and as a sheep before her shearers is dumb, so he openeth not his mouth.

CONDEMNATION

Romans 8:1 - [There is] therefore now no condemnation to them which are in Christ Jesus, who walk not after the flesh, but after the Spirit.

Romans 2:1 - Therefore thou art inexcusable, O man, whosoever thou art that judgest: for wherein thou judgest another, thou condemnest thyself; for thou that judgest doest the same things.

John 3:17 - For God sent not his Son into the world to condemn the world; but that the world through him might be saved.

1 John 3:20 - For if our heart condemn us, God is greater than our heart, and knoweth all things.

Romans 8:34 - Who [is] he that condemneth? [It is] Christ that died, yea rather, that is risen again, who is even at the right hand of God, who also maketh intercession for us.

CONFUSION

1 Corinthians 14:33 - For God is not [the author] of confusion, but of peace, as in all churches of the saints.

2 Timothy 2:7 - Consider what I say; and the Lord give thee understanding in all things.

1 John 4:1 - Beloved, believe not every spirit, but try the spirits whether they are of God: because many false prophets are gone out into the world.

Philippians 4:9 - Those things, which ye have both learned, and received, and heard, and seen in me, do: and the God of peace shall be with you.

Psalms 119:34 - Give me understanding, and I shall keep thy law; yea, I shall observe it with [my] whole heart.

Hebrews 13:8 - Jesus Christ the same yesterday, and to day, and for ever.

The Robe of Sins

John 16:13 - Howbeit when he, the Spirit of truth, is come, he will guide you into all truth: for he shall not speak of himself; but whatsoever he shall hear, [that] shall he speak: and he will shew you things to come.

Psalms 119:125 - I [am] thy servant; give me understanding, that I may know thy testimonies.

Proverbs 28:5 - Evil men understand not judgment: but they that seek the LORD understand all [things].

Deuteronomy 28:1 - And it shall come to pass, if thou shalt hearken diligently unto the voice of the LORD thy God, to observe [and] to do all his commandments which I command thee this day, that the LORD thy God will set thee on high above all nations of the earth:

CORRUPTION

2 Peter 2:19 - While they promise them liberty, they themselves are the servants of corruption: for of whom a man is overcome, of the same is he brought in bondage.

Galatians 6:8 - For he that soweth to his flesh shall of the flesh reap corruption; but he that soweth to the Spirit shall of the Spirit reap life everlasting.

2 Peter 1:4 - Whereby are given unto us exceeding great and precious promises: that by these ye might be partakers of the divine nature, having escaped the corruption that is in the world through lust.

John 16:33 - These things I have spoken unto you, that in me ye might have peace. In the world ye shall have tribulation: but be of good cheer; I have overcome the world.

Acts 2:27 - Because thou wilt not leave my soul in hell, neither wilt thou suffer thine Holy One to see corruption.

COVETOUS

Colossians 3:5 - Mortify therefore your members which are upon the earth; fornication, uncleanness, inordinate affection, evil concupiscence, and covetousness, which is idolatry:

Luke 12:15 - And he said unto them, Take heed, and beware of covetousness: for a man's life consisteth not in the abundance of the things which he possesseth.

Exodus 20:17 - Thou shalt not covet thy neighbour's house, thou shalt not covet thy neighbour's wife, nor his manservant, nor his maidservant, nor his ox, nor his ass, nor any thing that [is] thy neighbour's.

1 John 2:15 - Love not the world, neither the things [that are] in the world. If any man love the world, the love of the Father is not in him.

1 John 2:17 - And the world passeth away, and the lust thereof: but he that doeth the will of God abideth for ever.

James 4:2 - Ye lust, and have not: ye kill, and desire to have, and cannot obtain: ye fight and war, yet ye have not, because ye ask not.

CRIME

Romans 13:4 - For he is the minister of God to thee for good. But if thou do that which is evil, be afraid; for he beareth not the sword in vain: for he is the minister of God, a revenger to [execute] wrath upon him that doeth evil.

Exodus 22:1 - If a man shall steal an ox, or a sheep, and kill it, or sell it; he shall restore five oxen for an ox, and four sheep for a sheep.

Romans 13:1 - Let every soul be subject unto the higher powers. For there is no power but of God: the powers that be are ordained of God.

Genesis 9:5 - And surely your blood of your lives will I require; at the hand of every beast will I require it, and at the hand of man; at the hand of every man's brother will I require the life of man.

Exodus 22:2 - If a thief be found breaking up, and be smitten that he die, [there shall] no blood [be shed] for him.

CRITICIZING

James 4:11 - Speak not evil one of another, brethren. He that speaketh evil of [his] brother, and judgeth his brother, speaketh evil of the law, and judgeth the law: but if thou judge the law, thou art not a doer of the law, but a judge.

Romans 15:1 - We then that are strong ought to bear the infirmities of the weak, and not to please ourselves.

Romans 14:10 - But why dost thou judge thy brother? or why dost thou set at nought thy brother? for we shall all stand before the judgment seat of Christ.

Proverbs 26:12 - Seest thou a man wise in his own conceit? [there is] more hope of a fool than of him.

Colossians 3:12 - Put on therefore, as the elect of God, holy and beloved, bowels of mercies, kindness, humbleness of mind, meekness, longsuffering;

Proverbs 19:11 - The discretion of a man deferreth his anger; and [it is] his glory to pass over a transgression.

CROOKED

Deuteronomy 32:5 - They have corrupted themselves, their spot is not the spot of his children: they are a perverse and crooked generation.

Psalms 125:5 - As for such as turn aside unto their crooked ways, the LORD shall lead them forth with the workers of iniquity: but peace shall be upon Israel.

Proverbs 2:15 - Whose ways are crooked, and they froward in their paths:

Ecclesiastes 7:13 - Consider the work of God: for who can make that straight, which he hath made crooked?

Isaiah 42:16 - And I will bring the blind by a way that they knew not; I will lead them in paths that they have not known: I will make darkness light before them, and crooked things straight. These things will I do unto them, and not forsake them.

Isaiah 45:2 - I will go before thee, and make the crooked places straight: I will break in pieces the gates of brass, and cut in sunder the bars of iron:

Luke 3:5 - Every valley shall be filled, and every mountain and hill shall be brought low; and the crooked shall be made straight, and the rough ways shall be made smooth;

Philippians 2:15 - That ye may be blameless and harmless, the sons of God, without rebuke, in the midst of a crooked and perverse nation, among whom ye shine as lights in the world;

CURSING

Ephesians 5:4 - Neither filthiness, nor foolish talking, nor jesting, which are not convenient: but rather giving of thanks.

James 3:8 - But the tongue can no man tame; [it is] an unruly evil, full of deadly poison.

Colossians 3:8 - But now ye also put off all these; anger, wrath, malice, blasphemy, filthy communication out of your mouth.

Colossians 4:6 - Let your speech [be] alway with grace, seasoned with salt, that ye may know how ye ought to answer every man.

Luke 6:28 - Bless them that curse you, and pray for them which despitefully use you.

Romans 12:14 - Bless them which persecute you: bless, and curse not.

Matthew 15:18 - But those things which proceed out of the mouth come forth from the heart; and they defile the man.

Exodus 20:7 - Thou shalt not take the name of the LORD thy God in vain; for the LORD will not hold him guiltless that taketh his name in vain.

Matthew 15:11 - Not that which goeth into the mouth defileth a man; but that which cometh out of the mouth, this defileth a man.

DEATH

Proverbs 18:21 - Death and life [are] in the power of the tongue: and they that love it shall eat the fruit thereof.

Revelation 21:4 - And God shall wipe away all tears from their eyes; and there shall be no more death, neither sorrow, nor crying, neither shall there be any more pain: for the former things are passed away.

Acts 13:34 - And as concerning that he raised him up from the dead, [now] no more to return to corruption, he said on this wise, I will give you the sure mercies of David.

Romans 14:8 - For whether we live, we live unto the Lord; and whether we die, we die unto the Lord: whether we live therefore, or die, we are the Lord's.

Ecclesiastes 12:7 - Then shall the dust return to the earth as it was: and the spirit shall return unto God who gave it.

1 Thessalonians 4:14 - For if we believe that Jesus died and rose again, even so them also which sleep in Jesus will God bring with him.

John 3:16 - For God so loved the world, that he gave his only begotten Son, that whosoever believeth in him should not perish, but have everlasting life.

1 Corinthians 15:52 - In a moment, in the twinkling of an eye, at the last trumpet. For the trumpet shall sound, and the dead shall be raised incorruptible, and we shall be changed.

Romans 6:23 - For the wages of sin [is] death; but the gift of God [is] eternal life through Jesus Christ our Lord.

DECEITFUL

Psalms 5:6 - Thou shalt destroy them that speak leasing: the LORD will abhor the bloody and deceitful man.

Psalms 52:4 - Thou lovest all devouring words, O [thou] deceitful tongue.

Psalms 55:23 - But thou, O God, shalt bring them down into the pit of destruction: bloody and deceitful men shall not live out half their days; but I will trust in thee.

Proverbs 11:18 - The wicked worketh a deceitful work: but to him that soweth righteousness [shall be] a sure reward.

Proverbs 31:30 - Favour [is] deceitful, and beauty [is] vain: [but] a woman [that] feareth the LORD, she shall be praised.

Micah 6:11 - Shall I count [them] pure with the wicked balances, and with the bag of deceitful weights?

DEFEAT

Ephesians 6:10 - Finally, my brethren, be strong in the Lord, and in the power of his might.

Ephesians 6:12 - For we wrestle not against flesh and blood, but against principalities, against powers, against the rulers of the darkness of this world, against spiritual wickedness in high [places].

Ephesians 6:13 - Wherefore take unto you the whole armour of God, that ye may be able to withstand in the evil day, and having done all, to stand.

Ephesians 6:14 - Stand therefore, having your loins girt about with truth, and having on the breastplate of righteousness;

Ephesians 6:15 - And your feet shod with the preparation of the gospel of peace;

Ephesians 6:16 - Above all, taking the shield of faith, wherewith ye shall be able to quench all the fiery darts of the wicked.

Ephesians 6:17 - And take the helmet of salvation, and the sword of the Spirit, which is the word of God:

Ephesians 6:18 - Praying always with all prayer and supplication in the Spirit, and watching thereunto with all perseverance and supplication for all saints;

DEFILE

Numbers 5:14 - And the spirit of jealousy come upon him, and he be jealous of his wife, and she be defiled: or if the spirit of jealousy come upon him, and he be jealous of his wife, and she be not defiled:

Leviticus 11:44 - For I am the LORD your God: ye shall therefore sanctify yourselves, and ye shall be holy; for I am holy: neither shall ye defile yourselves with any manner of creeping thing that creepeth upon the earth.

Leviticus 18:20 - Moreover thou shalt not lie carnally with thy neighbour's wife, to deflie thyself with her.

Leviticus 18:23 - Neither shalt thou lie with any beast to defile thyself therewith: neither shall any woman stand before a beast to lie down thereto: it is confusion.

Leviticus 18:30 - Therefore shall ye keep mine ordinance, that ye commit not any one of these abominable customs, which were committed before you, and that ye deflie not yourselves therein: I am the LORD your God.

DELUSION

Isaiah 66:4 - "I also will choose their delusions, and will bring their fears upon them; because when I called, none did answer; when I spake, they did not hear: but they did evil before mine eyes, and chose that in which I delighted not."

2 Thessalonians 2:10 - ". . . because they received not the love of the truth, that they might be saved.

2 Thessalonians 2:11 - And for this cause God shall send them strong delusion, that they should believe a lie:"

2 Peter 3:5 (NASB) - For when they maintain this, it escapes their notice that by the word of God the heavens existed long ago and the earth was formed out of water and by water,

Luke 12:17 - And he thought within himself, saying, What shall I do, because I have no room where to bestow my fruits?

DEPRAVITY

Jeremiah 17:9 - The heart [is] deceitful above all [things], and desperately wicked: who can know it?

Psalms 51:5 - Behold, I was shapen in iniquity; and in sin did my mother conceive me.

Romans 7:18 - For I know that in me (that is, in my flesh,) dwelleth no good thing: for to will is present with me; but [how] to perform that which is good I find not.

Isaiah 64:6 - But we are all as an unclean [thing], and all our righteousnesses [are] as filthy rags; and we all do fade as a leaf; and our iniquities, like the wind, have taken us away.

1 Corinthians 2:14 - But the natural man receiveth not the things of the Spirit of God: for they are foolishness unto him: neither can he know [them], because they are spiritually discerned.

Psalms 58:3 - The wicked are estranged from the womb: they go astray as soon as they be born, speaking lies.

John 5:40 - And ye will not come to me, that ye might have life.

DESPAIR

Psalms 34:17 - [The righteous] cry, and the LORD heareth, and delivereth them out of all their troubles.

Romans 15:13 - Now the God of hope fill you with all joy and peace in believing, that ye may abound in hope, through the power of the Holy Ghost.

Philippians 4:19 - But my God shall supply all your need according to his riches in glory by Christ Jesus.

John 5:24 - Verily, verily, I say unto you, He that heareth my word, and believeth on him that sent me, hath everlasting life, and shall not come into condemnation; but is passed from death unto life.

Proverbs 30:5 - Every word of God [is] pure: he [is] a shield unto them that put their trust in him.

DESPERATE

Romans 15:13 - Now the God of hope fill you with all joy and peace in believing, that ye may abound in hope, through the power of the Holy Ghost.

1 John 4:18 - There is no fear in love; but perfect love casteth out fear: because fear hath torment. He that feareth is not made perfect in love.

1 Corinthians 15:33 - Be not deceived: evil communications corrupt good manners.

Jeremiah 29:10 - For thus saith the LORD, That after seventy years be accomplished at Babylon I will visit you, and perform my good word toward you, in causing you to return to this place.

Psalms 91:14 - Because he hath set his love upon me, therefore will I deliver him: I will set him on high, because he hath known my name.

DESPISE

Numbers 15:31 - Because he hath despised the word of the LORD, and hath broken his commandment, that soul shall utterly be cut off; his iniquity shall be upon him.

2 Samuel 6:16 - And as the ark of the LORD came into the city of David, Michal Saul's daughter looked through a window, and saw king David leaping and dancing before the LORD; and she despised him in her heart.

Job 5:17 - Behold, happy is the man whom God correcteth: therefore despised not thou the chastening of the Almighty:

Job 9:21 - Though I were perfect, yet would I not know my soul: I would despise my life.

Job 12:5 - He that is ready to slip with his feet is as a lamp despised in the thought of him that is at ease.

Job 19:18 - Yea, young children despised me; I arose, and they spake against me.

Job 36:5 - Behold, God is mighty, and despiseth not any: he is mighty in strength and wisdom.

DESTRUCTION

Luke 21:28 - And when these things begin to come to pass, then look up, and lift up your heads; for your redemption draweth nigh.

Matthew 24:42 - Watch therefore: for ye know not what hour your Lord doth come.

Proverbs 16:18 - Pride [goeth] before destruction, and an haughty spirit before a fall.

Luke 12:40 - Be ye therefore ready also: for the Son of man cometh at an hour when ye think not.

Revelation 13:13 - And he doeth great wonders, so that he maketh fire come down from heaven on the earth in the sight of men.

2 Peter 3:16 - as also in all his letters, speaking in them of these things, in which are some things hard to understand, which the untaught and unstable distort, as they do also the rest of the Scriptures, to their own destruction.

Proverbs 10:14 - Wise [men] lay up knowledge: but the mouth of the foolish [is] near destruction.

DISAPPOINTMENT

Psalms 121:1- I will lift up mine eyes unto the hills, from whence cometh my help.

Isaiah 40:28 - Hast thou not known? hast thou not heard, [that] the everlasting God, the LORD, the Creator of the ends of the earth, fainteth not, neither is weary? [there is] no searching of his understanding.

Isaiah 40:31 - But they that wait upon the LORD shall renew [their] strength; they shall mount up with wings as eagles; they shall run, and not be weary; [and] they shall walk, and not faint.

Hebrews 4:14 - Seeing then that we have a great high priest, that is passed into the heavens, Jesus the Son of God, let us hold fast [our] profession.

1 John 5:13 - These things have I written unto you that believe on the name of the Son of God; that ye may know that ye have eternal life, and

that ye may believe on the name of the Son of God.

Matthew 6:6 - But thou, when thou prayest, enter into thy closet, and when thou hast shut thy door, pray to thy Father which is in secret; and thy Father which seeth in secret shall reward thee openly.

Proverbs 23:18 - For surely there is an end; and thine expectation shall not be cut off.

Titus 2:13 - Looking for that blessed hope, and the glorious appearing of the great God and our Saviour Jesus Christ;

Habakkuk 2:3 - For the vision [is] yet for an appointed time, but at the end it shall speak, and not lie: though it tarry, wait for it; because it will surely come, it will not tarry.

DISCOURAGE

Galatians 6:9 - And let us not be weary in well doing: for in due season we shall reap, if we faint not.

Romans 15:13 - Now the God of hope fill you with all joy and peace in believing, that ye may abound in hope, through the power of the Holy Ghost.

2 Thessalonians 3:13 - But ye, brethren, be not weary in well doing.

James 4:7 - Submit yourselves therefore to God. Resist the devil, and he will flee from you.

John 5:30 - I can of mine own self do nothing: as I hear, I judge: and my judgment is just; because I seek not mine own will, but the will of the Father which hath sent me.

2 Timothy 2:4 - No man that warreth entangleth himself with the affairs of [this] life; that he may please him who hath chosen him to be a soldier.

DISOBEDIENCE

John 14:15 - If ye love me, keep my commandments.

Luke 6:46 - And why call ye me, Lord, Lord, and do not the things which I say?

Romans 3:23 - For all have sinned, and come short of the glory of God;

Acts 5:29 - Then Peter and the [other] apostles answered and said, We ought to obey God rather than men.

2 Chronicles 7:14 - If my people, which are called by my name, shall humble themselves, and pray, and seek my face, and turn from their wicked ways; then will I hear from heaven, and will forgive their sin, and will heal their land.

Matthew 22:37 - Jesus said unto him, Thou shalt love the Lord thy God with all thy heart, and with all thy soul, and with all thy mind.

Ephesians 2:2 - Wherein in time past ye walked according to the course of this world, according to the prince of the power of the air, the spirit that now work in the children of disobedience:

DISTRESS

2 Samuel 22:7 - In my distress I called upon the LORD, and cried to my God: and he did hear my voice out of his temple, and my cry [did enter] into his ears.

Psalms 4:1 - Hear me when I call, O God of my righteousness: thou hast enlarged me [when I was] in distress; have mercy upon me, and hear my prayer.

Psalms 118:5 - I called upon the LORD in distress: the LORD answered me, [and set me] in a large place.

Psalms 120:1 - A Song of degrees. In my distress I cried unto the LORD, and he heard me.

Proverbs 1:27 - When your fear cometh as desolation, and your destruction cometh as a whirlwind; when distress and anguish cometh upon you.

Isaiah 25:4 - For thou hast been a strength to the poor, a strength to the needy in his distress, a refuge from the storm, a shadow from the heat, when the blast of the terrible ones [is] as a storm [against] the wall.

Psalms 34:6 - This poor man cried, and the LORD heard [him], and saved him out of all his troubles.

Psalms 27:14 - Wait on the LORD: be of good courage, and he shall strengthen thine heart: wait, I say, on the LORD.

Psalms 91:1 - He that dwelleth in the secret place of the most High shall abide under the shadow of the Almighty.

Nahum 1:7 - The LORD [is] good, a strong hold in the day of trouble; and he knoweth them that trust in him.

Isaiah 65:24 - And it shall come to pass, that before they call, I will answer; and while they are yet speaking, I will hear.

Mark 5:36 - As soon as Jesus heard the word that was spoken, he saith unto the ruler of the synagogue, Be not afraid, only believe.

Deuteronomy 1:29 - Then I said unto you, Dread not, neither be afraid of them.

DIVISION

1 Corinthians 12:11 - But all these worketh that one and the selfsame Spirit, dividing to every man severally as he will.

Isaiah 63:12 - That led them by the right hand of Moses with his glorious arm, dividing the water before them, to make himself an everlasting name?

2 Timothy 2:15 - Study to shew thyself approved unto God, a workman that needeth not to be ashamed, rightly dividing the word of truth.

Hebrews 4:12 - For the word of God is quick, and powerful, and sharper than any two edged sword, piercing even to the dividing asunder of soul and spirit, and of the joints and marrow, and is a discerner of the thoughts and intents of the heart.

DOUBLE MINDEDNESS

James 1:6 - But let him ask in faith, nothing wavering. For he that wavereth is like a wave of the sea driven with the wind and tossed.

James 4:8 - Draw nigh to God, and he will draw nigh to you. Cleanse [your] hands, [ye] sinners; and purify [your] hearts, [ye] double minded.

James 1:8 - A double minded man [is] unstable in all his ways.

James 4:3 - Ye ask, and receive not, because ye ask amiss, that ye may consume [it] upon your lusts.

1 Peter 4:13 - But rejoice, inasmuch as ye are partakers of Christ's sufferings; that, when his glory shall be revealed, ye may be glad also with exceeding joy.

2 Corinthians 10:5 - Casting down imaginations, and every high thing that exalteth itself against

the knowledge of God, and bringing into captivity every thought to the obedience of Christ;

Galatians 5:16 - [This] I say then, Walk in the Spirit, and ye shall not fulfil the lust of the flesh.

DOUBT

James 1:6 - But let him ask in faith, nothing wavering. For he that wavereth is like a wave of the sea driven with the wind and tossed.

Matthew 21:21 - Jesus answered and said unto them, Verily I say unto you, If ye have faith, and doubt not, ye shall not only do this [which is done] to the fig tree, but also if ye shall say unto this mountain, Be thou removed, and be thou cast into the sea; it shall be done.

Matthew 14:31 - And immediately Jesus stretched forth [his] hand, and caught him, and said unto him, O thou of little faith, wherefore didst thou doubt?

Luke 24:38 - And he said unto them, Why are ye troubled? and why do thoughts arise in your hearts?

Mark 11:22 - And Jesus answering saith unto them, Have faith in God.

Hebrews 11:1 - Now faith is the substance of things hoped for, the evidence of things not seen.

John 20:27 - Then saith he to Thomas, Reach hither thy finger, and behold my hands; and reach hither thy hand, and thrust [it] into my side: and be not faithless, but believing.

Romans 14:23 - And he that doubteth is damned if he eat, because [he eateth] not of faith: for whatsoever [is] not of faith is sin.

DRUNKENNESS

Ephesians 5:18 - And be not drunk with wine, wherein is excess; but be filled with the Spirit;

Proverbs 20:1 - Wine [is] a mocker, strong drink [is] raging: and whosoever is deceived thereby is not wise.

Proverbs 23:30 - They that tarry long at the wine; they that go to seek mixed wine.

Romans 13:13 - Let us walk honestly, as in the day; not in rioting and drunkenness, not in chambering and wantonness, not in strife and envying.

Isaiah 28:7 - But they also have erred through wine, and through strong drink are out of the way; the priest and the prophet have erred through strong drink, they are swallowed up of wine, they are out of the way through strong drink; they err in vision, they stumble [in] judgment.

Proverbs 23:20 - Be not among winebibbers; among riotous eaters of flesh:

Titus 2:12 - Teaching us that, denying ungodliness and worldly lusts, we should live soberly, righteously, and godly, in this present world;

Isaiah 5:11 - Woe unto them that rise up early in the morning, [that] they may follow strong drink; that continue until night, [till] wine inflame them!

EFFEMINATE

Deuteronomy 22:5 - The woman shall not wear that which pertaineth unto a man, neither shall a man put on a woman's garment: for all that do so [are] abomination unto the LORD thy God.

Ezekiel 16:49 - Behold, this was the iniquity of thy sister Sodom, pride, fullness of bread, and abundance of idleness was in her and in her daughters, neither did she strengthen the hand of the poor and needy.

John 3:16 - For God so loved the world, that he gave his only begotten Son, that whosoever believeth in him should not perish, but have everlasting life.

John 3:17 - For God sent not his Son into the world to condemn the world; but that the world through him might be saved.

Luke 6:37 - Judge not, and ye shall not be judged: condemn not, and ye shall not be condemned: forgive, and ye shall be forgiven:

John 15:12 - This is my commandment, That ye love one another, as I have loved you.

ENEMIES

Proverbs 24:17 - Rejoice not when thine enemy falleth, and let not thine heart be glad when he stumbleth:

Romans 12:20 - Therefore if thine enemy hunger, feed him; if he thirst, give him drink: for in so doing thou shalt heap coals of fire on his head.

Matthew 5:44 – But I tell you, love your enemies and pray for those who persecute you.

Psalms 138:7 - Though I walk in the midst of trouble, thou wilt revive me: thou shalt stretch forth thine hand against the wrath of mine enemies, and thy right hand shall save me.

Proverbs 16:7 - When a man's ways please the LORD, he maketh even his enemies to be at peace with him.

Psalms 71:10 - For mine enemies speak against me; and they that lay wait for my soul take counsel together,

ENTICE

2 Chronicles 18:20 - Then there came out a spirit, and stood before the LORD, and said, I will entice him. And the LORD said unto him, Wherewith?

2 Chronicles 18:21 - And he said, I will go out, and be a lying spirit in the mouth of all his prophets. And the LORD said, Thou shalt entice him, and thou shalt also prevail: go out, and do even so.

Job 31:27 - And my heart hath been secretly enticed, or my mouth hath kissed my hand:

Proverbs 1:10 - My son, if sinners entice thee, consent thou not.

Proverbs 16:29 - A violent man enticeth his neighbour, and leadeth him into the way that is not good.

James 1:14 - But every man is tempted, when he is drawn away of his own lust, and enticed.

ENVY

Exodus 34:14 - For thou shalt worship no other god: for the LORD, whose name [is] Jealous, [is] a jealous God:

Proverbs 14:30 - A sound heart [is] the life of the flesh: but envy the rottenness of the bones.

Proverbs 23:17 - Let not thine heart envy sinners: but [be thou] in the fear of the LORD all the day long.

Galatians 5:26 - Let us not be desirous of vain glory, provoking one another, envying one another.

Proverbs 24:1 - Be not thou envious against evil men, neither desire to be with them.

1 Corinthians 13:4 - Charity suffereth long, [and] is kind; charity envieth not; charity vaunteth not itself, is not puffed up,

James 3:16 - For where envying and strife [is], there [is] confusion and every evil work.

Titus 3:3 - For we ourselves also were sometimes foolish, disobedient, deceived, serving divers lusts and pleasures, living in malice and envy, hateful, [and] hating one another.

EVILDOER

Proverbs 6:17 - A proud look, a lying tongue, and hands that shed innocent blood,

Proverbs 6:18 - A heart that deviseth wicked imaginations, feet that be swift in running to mischief,

Proverbs 6:19 - A false witness [that] speaketh lies, and he that soweth discord among brethren.

Psalms 37:1 - Fret not thyself because of evildoers, neither be thou envious against the workers of iniquity.

Luke 16:15 - And he said unto them, Ye are they which justify yourselves before men; but God knoweth your hearts: for that which is highly esteemed among men is abomination in the sight of God.

Matthew 7:22 - Many will say to me in that day, Lord, Lord, have we not prophesied in thy name?

and in thy name have cast out devils? and in thy name done many wonderful works?

Matthew 7:23 - And then will I profess unto them, I never knew you: depart from me, ye that work iniquity.

EXTORTION

Psalms 109:11 - Let the extortioner catch all that he hath; and let the strangers spoil his labour.

Ezekiel 22:12 - In thee have they taken gifts to shed blood; thou hast taken usury and increase, and thou hast greedily gained of thy neighbours by extortion, and hast forgotten me, saith the Lord GOD.

Matthew 23:25 - Woe unto you, scribes and Pharisees, hypocrites! for ye make clean the outside of the cup and of the platter, but within they are full of extortion and excess.

1 Corinthians 5:10 - Yet not altogether with the fornicators of this world, or with the covetous, or extortioner, or with idolaters; for then must ye needs go out of the world.

1 Corinthians 6:10 - Nor thieves, nor covetous, nor drunkards, nor revilers, nor extortioners, shall inherit the kingdom of God.

FAILURE

2 Corinthians 12:9 - And he said unto me, My grace is sufficient for thee: for my strength is made perfect in weakness. Most gladly therefore will I rather glory in my infirmities, that the power of Christ may rest upon me.

Psalms 73:26 - My flesh and my heart faileth: [but] God [is] the strength of my heart, and my portion for ever.

Proverbs 24:16 - For a just [man] falleth seven times, and riseth up again: but the wicked shall fall into mischief.

Proverbs 28:13 - He that covereth his sins shall not prosper: but whoso confesseth and forsaketh [them] shall have mercy.

Acts 22:16 - And now why tarriest thou? arise, and be baptized, and wash away thy sins, calling on the name of the Lord.

Psalms 37:24 - Though he fall, he shall not be utterly cast down: for the LORD upholdeth [him with] his hand.

FALSE WITNESS

Exodus 23:1 - Thou shalt not raise a false report: put not thine hand with the wicked to be an unrighteous witness.

Deuteronomy 19:18 - And the judges shall make diligent inquisition: and, behold, if the witness be a false witness, and hath testified falsely against his brother;

Mark 14:56 - For many bare false witness against him, but their witness agreed not together.

Exodus 20:16 - Thou shalt not bear false witness against thy neighbour.

Proverbs 6:19 - A false witness that speaketh lies, and he that soweth discord among brethren.

Matthew 26:59 - Now the chief priests, and elders, and all the council, sought false witness against Jesus, to put him to death;

Matthew 24:24 = For there shall arise false Christs, and false prophets, and shall shew great signs and wonders; insomuch that, if it were possible, they shall deceive the very elect.

Job 16:8 - And thou hast filled me with wrinkles, which is a witness against me: and my leanness rising up in me beareth witness to my face.

FEAR

Isaiah 41:10 - Fear thou not; for I [am] with thee: be not dismayed; for I [am] thy God: I will strengthen thee; yea, I will help thee; yea, I will uphold thee with the right hand of my righteousness.

2 Timothy 1:7 - For God hath not given us the spirit of fear; but of power, and of love, and of a sound mind.

1 John 4:18 - There is no fear in love; but perfect love casteth out fear: because fear hath torment. He that feareth is not made perfect in love.

Psalms 34:4 - I sought the LORD, and he heard me, and delivered me from all my fears.

Proverbs 29:25 - The fear of man bringeth a snare: but whoso putteth his trust in the LORD shall be safe.

Romans 8:15 - For ye have not received the spirit of bondage again to fear; but ye have received the Spirit of adoption, whereby we cry, Abba, Father.

Matthew 10:28 - And fear not them which kill the body, but are not able to kill the soul: but rather fear him which is able to destroy both soul and body in hell.

FOOLISH

Proverbs 18:2 - A fool hath no delight in understanding, but that his heart may discover itself.

Proverbs 1:7 - The fear of the LORD [is] the beginning of knowledge: [but] fools despise wisdom and instruction.

Proverbs 29:9 - [If] a wise man contendeth with a foolish man, whether he rage or laugh, [there is] no rest.

Psalms 14:1 - The fool hath said in his heart, [There is] no God. They are corrupt, they have done abominable works, [there is] none that doeth good.

Proverbs 18:7 - A fool's mouth [is] his destruction, and his lips [are] the snare of his soul.

Proverbs 15:7 - The lips of the wise disperse knowledge: but the heart of the foolish [doeth] not so.

Proverbs 14:9 - Fools make a mock at sin: but among the righteous [there is] favour.

Matthew 7:26 - And every one that heareth these sayings of mine, and doeth them not, shall be likened unto a foolish man, which built his house upon the sand:

Proverbs 26:3 - A whip for the horse, a bridle for the ass, and a rod for the fool's back.

Romans 1:22 - Professing themselves to be wise, they became fools,

FORNICATION

1 Corinthians 6:18 - Flee fornication. Every sin that a man doeth is without the body; but he that committeth fornication sinneth against his own body.

Galatians 5:19 - Now the works of the flesh are manifest, which are [these]; Adultery, fornication, uncleanness, lasciviousness,

1 Corinthians 7:2 - Nevertheless, [to avoid] fornication, let every man have his own wife, and let every woman have her own husband.

1 Corinthians 5:1 - It is reported commonly [that there is] fornication among you, and such fornication as is not so much as named among the Gentiles, that one should have his father's wife.

1 Corinthians 6:13 - Meats for the belly, and the belly for meats: but God shall destroy both it and them. Now the body [is] not for fornication, but for the Lord; and the Lord for the body.

1 Thessalonians 4:3 - For this is the will of God, [even] your sanctification, that ye should abstain from fornication:

FRAUD

Leviticus 19:13 - Thou shalt not defraud thy neighbour, neither rob him: the wages of him that is hired shall not abide with thee all night until the morning.

1 Samuel 12:4 - And they said, Thou hast not defrauded us, nor oppressed us, neither hast thou taken ought of any man's hand.

1 Corinthians 7:5 – Defraud ye not one the other, except it be with consent for a time, that ye may give yourselves to fasting and prayer; and come together again, that Satan tempt you not for your incontinency.

2 Corinthians 7:2 - Receive us; we have wronged no man, we have corrupted no man, we have defrauded no man.

1 Thessalonians 4:6 - That no man go beyond and defraud his brother in any matter: because

that the Lord is the avenger of all such, as we also have forewarned you and testified.

FRUSTRATION

Isaiah 41:10 - Fear thou not; for I [am] with thee: be not dismayed; for I [am] thy God: I will strengthen thee; yea, I will help thee; yea, I will uphold thee with the right hand of my righteousness.

John 16:33 - These things I have spoken unto you, that in me ye might have peace. In the world ye shall have tribulation: but be of good cheer; I have overcome the world.

Galatians 6:9 - And let us not be weary in well doing: for in due season we shall reap, if we faint not.

Psalms 4:4-5 - Stand in awe, and sin not: commune with your own heart upon your bed, and be still. Selah.

Philippians 4:7 - And the peace of God, which passeth all understanding, shall keep your hearts and minds through Christ Jesus.

Proverbs 3:6 - In all thy ways acknowledge him, and he shall direct thy paths.

Exodus 14:14 - The LORD shall fight for you, and ye shall hold your peace.

Psalms 62:5 - My soul, wait thou only upon God; for my expectation [is] from him.

Psalms 62:6 - He only [is] my rock and my salvation: [he is] my defence; I shall not be moved.

Psalms 62:7 - In God [is] my salvation and my glory: the rock of my strength, [and] my refuge, [is] in God.

Proverbs 3:5 - Trust in the LORD with all thine heart; and lean not unto thine own understanding.

GAMBLING

Ephesians 4:28 - Let him that stole steal no more: but rather let him labour, working with [his] hands the thing which is good, that he may have to give to him that needeth.

Proverbs 28:22 - He that hasteth to be rich [hath] an evil eye, and considereth not that poverty shall come upon him.

Proverbs 16:33 - The lot is cast into the lap; but the whole disposing thereof [is] of the LORD.

1 Corinthians 6:12 - All things are lawful unto me, but all things are not expedient: all things are lawful for me, but I will not be brought under the power of any.

Acts 20:35 - I have shewed you all things, how that so labouring ye ought to support the weak, and to remember the words of the Lord Jesus, how he said, It is more blessed to give than to receive.

Matthew 6:20 - But lay up for yourselves treasures in heaven, where neither moth nor rust doth corrupt, and where thieves do not break through nor steal:

Luke 12:34 - For where your treasure is, there will your heart be also.

1 Timothy 6:19 - Laying up in store for themselves a good foundation against the time to come, that they may lay hold on eternal life.

GOSSIP

Proverbs 16:28 - A froward man soweth strife: and a whisperer separateth chief friends.

Proverbs 21:23 - Whoso keepeth his mouth and his tongue keepeth his soul from troubles.

James 1:26 - If any man among you seem to be religious, and bridleth not his tongue, but deceiveth his own heart, this man's religion [is] vain.

Proverbs 20:19 - He that goeth about [as] a talebearer revealeth secrets: therefore meddle not with him that flattereth with his lips.

Psalms 34:13 - Keep thy tongue from evil, and thy lips from speaking guile.

Titus 3:2 - To speak evil of no man, to be no brawlers, [but] gentle, shewing all meekness unto all men.

The Robe of Sins

Proverbs 18:8 - The words of a talebearer [are] as wounds, and they go down into the innermost parts of the belly.

Proverbs 17:4 - A wicked doer giveth heed to false lips; [and] a liar giveth ear to a naughty tongue.

Proverbs 11:13 - A talebearer revealeth secrets: but he that is of a faithful spirit concealeth the matter.

1 Timothy 5:13 - And withal they learn [to be] idle, wandering about from house to house; and not only idle, but tattlers also and busybodies, speaking things which they ought not.

Proverbs 17:9 - He that covereth a transgression seeketh love; but he that repeateth a matter separateth [very] friends.

GREED

Hebrews 13:5 - [Let your] conversation [be] without covetousness; [and be] content with such things as ye have: for he hath said, I will never leave thee, nor forsake thee.

Proverbs 15:27 - He that is greedy of gain troubleth his own house; but he that hateth gifts shall live.

1 John 2:15 - Love not the world, neither the things [that are] in the world. If any man love the world, the love of the Father is not in him.

2 Corinthians 9:7 - Every man according as he purposeth in his heart, [so let him give]; not grudgingly, or of necessity: for God loveth a cheerful giver.

Acts 20:35 - I have shewed you all things, how that so labouring ye ought to support the weak, and to remember the words of the Lord Jesus, how he said, It is more blessed to give than to receive.

1 Timothy 6:10 - For the love of money is the root of all evil: which while some coveted after, they have erred from the faith, and pierced themselves through with many sorrows.

Luke 12:15 - And he said unto them, Take heed, and beware of covetousness: for a man's life consisteth not in the abundance of the things which he possesseth.

Matthew 6:24 - No man can serve two masters: for either he will hate the one, and love the other; or else he will hold to the one, and despise the other. Ye cannot serve God and mammon.

Proverbs 20:21 - An inheritance [may be] gotten hastily at the beginning; but the end thereof shall not be blessed.

James 5:1 - Go to now, [ye] rich men, weep and howl for your miseries that shall come upon [you].

James 5:2 (NIV) – Your wealth has rotted, and moths have eaten your clothes.

Matthew 6:33 - But seek ye first the kingdom of God, and his righteousness; and all these things shall be added unto you.

Proverbs 21:26 - He coveteth greedily all the day long: but the righteous giveth and spareth not.

GRIEF

Matthew 5:4 - Blessed [are] they that mourn: for they shall be comforted.

Revelation 21:4 - And God shall wipe away all tears from their eyes; and there shall be no more death, neither sorrow, nor crying, neither shall there be any more pain: for the former things are passed away.

Psalms 56:8 - Thou tell my wanderings: put thou my tears into thy bottle: [are they] not in thy book?

Psalms 31:9 - Have mercy upon me, O LORD, for I am in trouble: mine eye is consumed with grief, [yea], my soul and my belly.

1 Thessalonians 4:13 - But I would not have you to be ignorant, brethren, concerning them which are asleep, that ye sorrow not, even as others which have no hope.

John 11:35 - Jesus wept.

GRUDGE

Romans 12:17 - Recompense to no man evil for evil. Provide things honest in the sight of all men.

Mark 11:25 - And when ye stand praying, forgive, if ye have ought against any: that your Father also which is in heaven may forgive you your trespasses.

Ephesians 4:32 - And be ye kind one to another, tenderhearted, forgiving one another, even as God for Christ's sake hath forgiven you.

Leviticus 19:18 - Thou shalt not avenge, nor bear any grudge against the children of thy people, but thou shalt love thy neighbor as thyself: I [am] the LORD.

Luke 17:3 - Take heed to yourselves: If thy brother trespass against thee, rebuke him; and if he repent, forgive him.

Matthew 7:1- Judge not, that ye be not judged.

GUILT

1 John 1:9 - If we confess our sins, he is faithful and just to forgive us [our] sins, and to cleanse us from all unrighteousness.

Romans 8:1 - [There is] therefore now no condemnation to them which are in Christ Jesus, who walk not after the flesh, but after the Spirit.

Romans 5:1 - Therefore being justified by faith, we have peace with God through our Lord Jesus Christ:

Romans 10:13 - For whosoever shall call upon the name of the Lord shall be saved.

1 John 2:1 - My little children, these things write I unto you, that ye sin not. And if any man sin, we have an advocate with the Father, Jesus Christ the righteous:

2 Peter 3:9 - The Lord is not slack concerning his promise, as some men count slackness; but

is longsuffering to us-ward, not willing that any should perish, but that all should come to repentance.

HARASSMENT

Leviticus 19:18 - Thou shalt not avenge, nor bear any grudge against the children of thy people, but thou shalt love thy neighbour as thyself: I [am] the LORD.

Deuteronomy 31:6 - Be strong and of a good courage, fear not, nor be afraid of them: for the LORD thy God, he [it is] that doth go with thee; he will not fail thee, nor forsake thee.

1 John 2:9 - He that saith he is in the light, and hateth his brother, is in darkness even until now.

Psalms 18:3 - I will call upon the LORD, [who is worthy] to be praised: so shall I be saved from mine enemies.

Isaiah 41:11 - Behold, all they that were incensed against thee shall be ashamed and confounded: they shall be as nothing; and they that strive with thee shall perish.

HATE

John 15:18 - If the world hate you, ye know that it hated me before [it hated] you.

1 John 4:20 - If a man say, I love God, and hate his brother, he is a liar: for he that love not his brother whom he hath seen, how can he love God whom he hath not seen?

Proverbs 10:12 - Hatred stirred up strife: but love covered all sins.

1 John 3:15 - Whosoever hate his brother is a murderer: and ye know that no murderer hath eternal life abiding in him.

1 John 2:9 - He that said he is in the light, and hates his brother, is in darkness even until now.

Matthew 6:24 - No man can serve two masters: for either he will hate the one, and love the other; or else he will hold to the one, and despise the other. Ye cannot serve God and mammon.

Proverbs 8:13 - The fear of the LORD [is] to hate evil: pride, and arrogancy, and the evil way, and the froward mouth, do I hate.

HEARTACHE

Proverbs 3:4- So shalt thou find favour and good understanding in the sight of God and man.

Nahum 1:7 - The LORD [is] good, a strong hold in the day of trouble; and he knoweth them that trust in him.

Philippians 4:13 - I can do all things through Christ which strengtheneth me.

John 15:13 - Greater love hath no man than this, that a man lay down his life for his friends.

Proverbs 15:13 - A merry heart maketh a cheerful countenance: but by sorrow of the heart the spirit is broken.

HEARTBREAK

Psalms 147:3 - He healeth the broken in heart, and bindeth up their wounds.

Psalms 34:18 - The LORD [is] nigh unto them that are of a broken heart; and saveth such as be of a contrite spirit.

Proverbs 14:13 - Even in laughter the heart is sorrowful; and the end of that mirth [is] heaviness.

Proverbs 12:25 - Heaviness in the heart of man maketh it stoop: but a good word maketh it glad.

2 Chronicles 7:14 - If my people, which are called by my name, shall humble themselves, and pray, and seek my face, and turn from their wicked ways; then will I hear from heaven, and will forgive their sin, and will heal their land.

Proverbs 3:5 - Trust in the LORD with all thine heart; and lean not unto thine own understanding.

Proverbs 13:12 - Hope deferred maketh the heart sick: but [when] the desire cometh, [it is] a tree of life.

HOMOSEXUALITY

Leviticus 18:22 - Thou shalt not lie with mankind, as with womankind: it [is] abomination.

1 Corinthians 6:9 - Know ye not that the unrighteous shall not inherit the kingdom of God? Be not deceived: neither fornicators, nor idolaters, nor adulterers, nor effeminate, nor abusers of themselves with mankind,

Leviticus 20:13 - If a man also lie with mankind, as he lieth with a woman, both of them have committed an abomination: they shall surely be put to death; their blood [shall be] upon them.

Romans 1:26 - For this cause God gave them up unto vile affections: for even their women did change the natural use into that which is against nature:

1 Timothy 1:10 - For whoremongers, for them that defile themselves with mankind, for menstealers, for liars, for perjured persons, and if

The Robe of Sins

there be any other thing that is contrary to sound doctrine;

Mark 10:6 - But from the beginning of the creation God made them male and female.

Jude 1:7 - Even as Sodom and Gomorrha, and the cities about them in like manner, giving themselves over to fornication, and going after strange flesh, are set forth for an example, suffering the vengeance of eternal fire.

Romans 1:27 - And likewise also the men, leaving the natural use of the woman, burned in their lust one toward another; men with men working that which is unseemly, and receiving in themselves that recompence of their error which was meet.

Romans 1:32 - Who knowing the judgment of God, that they which commit such things are worthy of death, not only do the same, but have pleasure in them that do them.

HYPOCRITE

Matthew 6:1 - Take heed that ye do not your alms before men, to be seen of them: otherwise ye have no reward of your Father which is in heaven.

Matthew 7:5 - Thou hypocrite, first cast out the beam out of thine own eye; and then shalt thou see clearly to cast out the mote out of thy brother's eye.

2 Corinthians 11:14 - And no marvel; for Satan himself is transformed into an angel of light.

James 1:26 - If any man among you seem to be religious, and bridleth not his tongue, but deceiveth his own heart, this man's religion [is] vain.

Matthew 23:27 - Woe unto you, scribes and Pharisees, hypocrites! for ye are like unto whited sepulchres, which indeed appear beautiful outward, but are within full of dead [men's] bones, and of all uncleanness.

James 2:14 - What [doth it] profit, my brethren, though a man say he hath faith, and have not works? can faith save him?

2 Thessalonians 3:6 - Now we command you, brethren, in the name of our Lord Jesus Christ, that ye withdraw yourselves from every brother that walketh disorderly, and not after the tradition which he received of us.

IDOL

Exodus 20:3 - Thou shalt have no other gods before me.

Psalms 135:15 - The idols of the heathen [are] silver and gold, the work of men's hands.

Isaiah 37:19 - And have cast their gods into the fire: for they [were] no gods, but the work of men's hands, wood and stone: therefore they have destroyed them.

Habakkuk 2:18 - What profiteth the graven image that the maker thereof hath graven it; the molten image, and a teacher of lies, that the maker of his work trusteth therein, to make dumb idols?

Leviticus 26:1 - Ye shall make you no idols nor graven image, neither rear you up a standing image, neither shall ye set up [any] image of stone in your land, to bow down unto it: for I [am] the LORD your God.

Colossians 2:8 - Beware lest any man spoil you through philosophy and vain deceit, after the tradition of men, after the rudiments of the world, and not after Christ.

Ezekiel 20:32 - And that which cometh into your mind shall not be at all, that ye say, We will be as the heathen, as the families of the countries, to serve wood and stone.

1 John 5:21 - Little children, keep yourselves from idols. Amen.

IGNORANCE

Ephesians 4:18 - Having the understanding darkened, being alienated from the life of God through the ignorance that is in them, because of the blindness of their heart:

Hosea 4:6 - My people are destroyed for lack of knowledge: because thou hast rejected knowledge, I will also reject thee, that thou shalt be no priest to me: seeing thou hast forgotten the law of thy God, I will also forget thy children.

Acts 17:30 - And the times of this ignorance God winked at; but now commandeth all men everywhere to repent:

Luke 23:34 - Then said Jesus, Father, forgive them; for they know not what they do. And they parted his raiment, and cast lots.

The Robe of Sins

John 13:7 - Jesus answered and said unto him, What I do thou knowest not now; but thou shalt know hereafter.

IMMORALITY

Mark 7:20 - And he said, That which cometh out of the man, that defileth the man.

Colossians 3:5 - Mortify therefore your members which are upon the earth; fornication, uncleanness, inordinate affection, evil concupiscence, and covetousness, which is idolatry:

Proverbs 7:1 - My son, keep my words, and lay up my commandments with thee.

Genesis 2:24 - Therefore shall a man leave his father and his mother, and shall cleave unto his wife: and they shall be one flesh.

Ezekiel 18:20 - The soul that sinneth, it shall die. The son shall not bear the iniquity of the father, neither shall the father bear the iniquity of the son: the righteousness of the righteous shall be upon him, and the wickedness of the wicked shall be upon him.

The Robe of Sins

Jeremiah 31:34 - And they shall teach no more every man his neighbour, and every man his brother, saying, Know the LORD: for they shall all know me, from the least of them unto the greatest of them, saith the LORD: for I will forgive their iniquity, and I will remember their sin no more.

INJUSTICE

Proverbs 17:15 - He that justifieth the wicked, and he that condemneth the just, even they both [are] abomination to the LORD.

Ecclesiastes 5:8 - If thou seest the oppression of the poor, and violent perverting of judgment and justice in a province, marvel not at the matter: for [he that is] higher than the highest regardeth; and [there be] higher than they.

Psalms 43:1 - Judge me, O God, and plead my cause against an ungodly nation: O deliver me from the deceitful and unjust man.

Proverbs 29:27 - An unjust man [is] an abomination to the just: and [he that is] upright in the way [is] abomination to the wicked.

Exodus 23:7 - Keep thee far from a false matter; and the innocent and righteous slay thou not: for I will not justify the wicked.

Job 5:8 - I would seek unto God, and unto God would I commit my cause:

Psalms 82:2 - How long will ye judge unjustly, and accept the persons of the wicked? Selah.

INSANITY

John 10:20 - And many of them said, He hath a devil, and is mad; why hear ye him?

Mark 3:21 - And when his friends heard [of it], they went out to lay hold on him: for they said, He is beside himself.

1 Samuel 18:10 - And it came to pass on the morrow, that the evil spirit from God came upon Saul, and he prophesied in the midst of the house: and David played with his hand, as at other times: and [there was] a javelin in Saul's hand.

Matthew 7:6 - Give not that which is holy unto the dogs, neither cast ye your pearls before swine, lest they trample them under their feet, and turn again and rend you.

Luke 8:35 - Then they went out to see what was done; and came to Jesus, and found the man, out of whom the devils were departed, sitting at the feet of Jesus, clothed, and in his right mind: and they were afraid.

Acts 26:24 - And as he thus spake for himself, Festus said with a loud voice, Paul, thou art beside thyself; much learning doth make thee mad.

Acts 26:25 - But he said, I am not mad, most noble Festus; but speak forth the words of truth and soberness.

INTIMIDATION

2 Corinthians 11:20 - For ye suffer, if a man bring you into bondage, if a man devour [you], if a man take [of you], if a man exalt himself, if a man smite you on the face.

James 5:16 - Confess [your] faults one to another, and pray one for another, that ye may be healed. The effectual fervent prayer of a righteous man availeth much.

Galatians 6:12 - As many as desire to make a fair shew in the flesh, they constrain you to be circumcised; only lest they should suffer persecution for the cross of Christ.

John 8:32 - And ye shall know the truth, and the truth shall make you free.

Deuteronomy 31:6 - Be strong and of a good courage, fear not, nor be afraid of them: for the LORD thy God, he [it is] that doth go with thee; he will not fail thee, nor forsake thee.

JEALOUSY

James 3:16 - For where envying and strife [is], there [is] confusion and every evil work.

Proverbs 27:4 - Wrath [is] cruel, and anger [is] outrageous; but who [is] able to stand before envy?

Galatians 5:21 - Envyings, murders, drunkenness, revellings, and such like: of the which I tell you before, as I have also told [you] in time past, that they which do such things shall not inherit the kingdom of God.

Job 5:2 - For wrath killeth the foolish man, and envy slayeth the silly one.

2 Corinthians 11:2 - For I am jealous over you with godly jealousy: for I have espoused you to one husband, that I may present [you as] a chaste virgin to Christ.

Matthew 5:28 - But I say unto you, That whosoever looketh on a woman to lust after her hath committed adultery with her already in his heart.

LAZINESS

Proverbs 13:4 - The soul of the sluggard desireth, and [hath] nothing: but the soul of the diligent shall be made fat.

Colossians 3:23 - And whatsoever ye do, do [it] heartily, as to the Lord, and not unto men;

2 Thessalonians 3:10 - For even when we were with you, this we commanded you, that if any would not work, neither should he eat.

Proverbs 18:9 - He also that is slothful in his work is brother to him that is a great waster.

Proverbs 20:13 - Love not sleep, lest thou come to poverty; open thine eyes, [and] thou shalt be satisfied with bread.

Proverbs 19:15 - Slothfulness casteth into a deep sleep; and an idle soul shall suffer hunger.

Proverbs 26:13 - The slothful [man] saith, [There is] a lion in the way; a lion [is] in the streets.

2 Thessalonians 3:11 - For we hear that there are some which walk among you disorderly, working not at all, but are busybodies.

LIAR

Proverbs 19:9 - A false witness shall not be unpunished, and [he that] speaketh lies shall perish.

John 8:44 - Ye are of [your] father the devil, and the lusts of your father ye will do. He was a murderer from the beginning, and abode not in the truth, because there is no truth in him. When he speaketh a lie, he speaketh of his own: for he is a liar, and the father of it.

Proverbs 14:5 - A faithful witness will not lie: but a false witness will utter lies.

James 3:14 - But if ye have bitter envying and strife in your hearts, glory not, and lie not against the truth.

2 Corinthians 11:13 - For such [are] false apostles, deceitful workers, transforming themselves into the apostles of Christ.

Proverbs 14:25 - A true witness delivereth souls: but a deceitful [witness] speaketh lies.

Psalms 120:2 - Deliver my soul, O LORD, from lying lips, [and] from a deceitful tongue

LOSS

2 Corinthians 1:3 - Blessed [be] God, even the Father of our Lord Jesus Christ, the Father of mercies, and the God of all comfort;

1 Thessalonians 4:14 - For if we believe that Jesus died and rose again, even so them also which sleep in Jesus will God bring with him.

Ecclesiastes 3:4 - A time to weep, and a time to laugh; a time to mourn, and a time to dance;

1 Thessalonians 4:13 - But I would not have you to be ignorant, brethren, concerning them which are asleep, that ye sorrow not, even as others which have no hope.

John 11:25 - Jesus said unto her, I am the resurrection, and the life: he that believeth in me, though he were dead, yet shall he live:

Colossians 1:13 - Who hath delivered us from the power of darkness, and hath translated [us] into the kingdom of his dear Son:

LUST

Galatians 5:16 - [This] I say then, Walk in the Spirit, and ye shall not fulfil the lust of the flesh.

1 John 2:16 - For all that [is] in the world, the lust of the flesh, and the lust of the eyes, and the pride of life, is not of the Father, but is of the world.

2 Timothy 2:22 - Flee also youthful lusts: but follow righteousness, faith, charity, peace, with them that call on the Lord out of a pure heart.

1 Peter 2:11 - Dearly beloved, I beseech [you] as strangers and pilgrims, abstain from fleshly lusts, which war against the soul;

James 1:15 – Then when lust hath conceived, it bringeth forth sin: and sin, when it is finished, bringeth forth death.

Jude 1:18 - How that they told you there should be mockers in the last time, who should walk after their own ungodly lusts.

MALICE

Ephesians 4:31 - Let all bitterness, and wrath, and anger, and clamour, and evil speaking, be put away from you, with all malice:

Titus 3:3 - For we also once were foolish ourselves, disobedient, deceived, enslaved to various lusts and pleasures, spending our life in malice and envy, hateful, hating one another.

1 Peter 2:16 - Act as free men, and do not use your freedom as a covering for maliciousness, but use it as servants of God.

1 Peter 2:1 (NIV) - Therefore, putting aside all malice and all deceit and hypocrisy and envy and all slander,

Romans 1:29 (ESV)- being filled with all unrighteousness, wickedness, greed, evil; full of envy, murder, strife, deceit, malice; they are gossips,

MANIPULATION

2 Corinthians 11:14 (ESV)- And no wonder, for even Satan disguises himself as an angel of light.

Galatians 1:8-9 - But though we, or an angel from heaven, preach any other gospel unto you than that which we have preached unto you, let him be accursed. As we said before, so say I now again, if any man preach any other gospel unto you than that ye have received, let him be accursed.

Matthew 7:15 (NLT) - Beware of false prophets who come disguised as harmless sheep but are really vicious wolves.

Romans 16:18 (NLT)- Such people are not serving Christ our Lord; they are serving their own personal interests. By smooth talk and glowing words they deceive innocent people.

2 Peter 2:1 (ESV)- But false prophets also arose among the people, just as there will be false

teachers among you, who will secretly bring in destructive heresies, even denying the Master who bought them, bringing upon themselves swift destruction.

Luke 16:15 (NIV)- He said to them, "You are the ones who justify yourselves in the eyes of others, but God knows your hearts. What people value highly is detestable in God's sight.

MASTURBATION

1 Corinthians 6:18 - Flee fornication. Every sin that a man doeth is without the body; but he that committeth fornication sinneth against his own body.

1 Thessalonians 4:3 - For this is the will of God, [even] your sanctification, that ye should abstain from fornication:

Colossians 3:5 - Mortify therefore your members which are upon the earth; fornication, uncleanness, inordinate affection, evil concupiscence, and covetousness, which is idolatry:

1 Corinthians 7:3 - Let the husband render unto the wife due benevolence: and likewise also the wife unto the husband.

Leviticus 15:16 - And if any man's seed of copulation go out from him, then he shall wash all his flesh in water, and be unclean until the even.

Romans 13:14 - But put ye on the Lord Jesus Christ, and make not provision for the flesh, to [fulfil] the lusts [thereof].

MISERY

Judges 10:16 - And they put away the strange gods from among them, and served the LORD: and his soul was grieved for the misery of Israel.

Job 3:20 - Wherefore is light given to him that is in misery, and life unto the bitter in soul;

Job 11:16 - Because thou shalt forget thy misery, and remember it as waters that pass away:

Proverbs 31:7 - Let him drink, and forget his poverty, and remember his misery no more.

Ecclesiastes 8:6 - Because to every purpose there is time and judgment, therefore the misery of man is great upon him.

Lamentations 3:19 - Remembering mine affliction and my misery, the wormwood and the gall.

MOCKERY

Proverbs 17:5 - Whoso mocketh the poor reproacheth his Maker: [and] he that is glad at calamities shall not be unpunished.

Proverbs 15:12 - A scorner loveth not one that reproveth him: neither will he go unto the wise.

Isaiah 57:4 - Against whom do ye sport yourselves? against whom make ye a wide mouth, [and] draw out the tongue? [are] ye not children of transgression, a seed of falsehood,

Galatians 6:7 - Be not deceived; God is not mocked: for whatsoever a man soweth, that shall he also reap.

Psalms 1:1 - Blessed [is] the man that walketh not in the counsel of the ungodly, nor standeth in the way of sinners, nor sitteth in the seat of the scornful.

MISTAKE

Proverbs 28:13 - He that covereth his sins shall not prosper: but whoso confesseth and forsaketh [them] shall have mercy.

Ephesians 5:8 - For ye were sometimes darkness, but now [are ye] light in the Lord: walk as children of light:

2 Timothy 3:16 - All scripture [is] given by inspiration of God, and [is] profitable for doctrine, for reproof, for correction, for instruction in righteousness:

Deuteronomy 28:1 - And it shall come to pass, if thou shalt hearken diligently unto the voice of the LORD thy God, to observe [and] to do all his commandments which I command thee this day, that the LORD thy God will set thee on high above all nations of the earth:

1 Peter 2:9 - But ye [are] a chosen generation, a royal priesthood, an holy nation, a peculiar

people; that ye should shew forth the praises of him who hath called you out of darkness into his marvellous light:

MURDER

Leviticus 24:17 - And he that killeth any man shall surely be put to death.

Exodus 20:13 - Thou shalt not kill.

Matthew 5:21 - Ye have heard that it was said by them of old time, Thou shalt not kill; and whosoever shall kill shall be in danger of the judgment:

1 John 3:12 - Not as Cain, [who] was of that wicked one, and slew his brother. And wherefore slew he him? Because his own works were evil, and his brother's righteous.

1 John 3:15 - Whosoever hateth his brother is a murderer: and ye know that no murderer hath eternal life abiding in him.

Revelation 21:8 - But the fearful, and unbelieving, and the abominable, and murderers, and whoremongers, and sorcerers, and idolaters, and all liars, shall have their part in the lake which burneth with fire and brimstone: which is the second death.

Deuteronomy 5:17 - Thou shalt not kill.

NEGLECT

Matthew 18:17 - And if he shall neglect to hear them, tell it unto the church: but if he neglect to hear the church, let him be unto thee as an heathen man and a publican.

Acts 6:1 - And in those days, when the number of the disciples was multiplied, there arose a murmuring of the Grecians against the Hebrews, because their widows were neglected in the daily ministration.

Colossians 2:23 - Which things have indeed a shew of wisdom in will worship, and humility, and neglecting of the body; not in any honour to the satisfying of the flesh.

1 Timothy 4:14 - Neglect not the gift that is in thee, which was given thee by prophecy, with the laying on of the hands of the presbytery.

Hebrews 2:3 - How shall we escape, if we neglect so great salvation; which at the first began to be spoken by the Lord, and was confirmed unto us by them that heard him;

OCCULTISM

Leviticus 20:6 - And the soul that turneth after such as have familiar spirits, and after wizards, to go a whoring after them, I will even set my face against that soul, and will cut him off from among his people.

Deuteronomy 18:9 - When thou art come into the land which the LORD thy God giveth thee, thou shalt not learn to do after the abominations of those nations.

Galatians 5:19 - Now the works of the flesh are manifest, which are [these]; Adultery, fornication, uncleanness, lasciviousness,

Acts 19:19 - Many of them also which used curious arts brought their books together, and burned them before all [men]: and they counted the price of them, and found [it] fifty thousand [pieces] of silver.

Leviticus 20:27 - A man also or woman that hath a familiar spirit, or that is a wizard, shall surely be put to death: they shall stone them with stones: their blood [shall be] upon them.

OFFEND

2 Chronicles 28:13 - And said unto them, Ye shall not bring in the captives hither: for whereas we have offended against the LORD already, ye intend to add more to our sins and to our trespass: for our trespass is great, and there is fierce wrath against Israel.

Job 34:31 - Surely it is meet to be said unto God, I have borne chastisement, I will not offend any more:

Psalms 73:15 - If I say, I will speak thus; behold, I should offend against the generation of thy children.

Psalms 119:165 - Great peace have they which love thy law: and nothing shall offend them.

Proverbs 18:19 - A brother offended is harder to be won than a strong city: and their contentions are like the bars of a castle.

OPPRESSION

Psalms 9:9 - The LORD also will be a refuge for the oppressed, a refuge in times of trouble.

Proverbs 14:31 - He that oppresseth the poor reproacheth his Maker: but he that honoureth him hath mercy on the poor.

Isaiah 1:17 - Learn to do well; seek judgment, relieve the oppressed, judge the fatherless, plead for the widow.

Psalms 72:4 - He shall judge the poor of the people, he shall save the children of the needy, and shall break in pieces the oppressor.

Zechariah 7:10 - And oppress not the widow, nor the fatherless, the stranger, nor the poor; and let none of you imagine evil against his brother in your heart.

Psalms 146:7 - Which executeth judgment for the oppressed: which giveth food to the hungry. The LORD looseth the prisoners:

James 2:6 - But ye have despised the poor. Do not rich men oppress you, and draw you before the judgment seats?

PAIN

Revelation 21:4 - And God shall wipe away all tears from their eyes; and there shall be no more death, neither sorrow, nor crying, neither shall there be any more pain: for the former things are passed away.

Romans 8:18 - For I reckon that the sufferings of this present time [are] not worthy [to be compared] with the glory which shall be revealed in us.

1 Peter 4:12 - Beloved, think it not strange concerning the fiery trial which is to try you, as though some strange thing happened unto you:

Psalms 41:3 - The LORD will strengthen him upon the bed of languishing: thou wilt make all his bed in his sickness.

Job 14:22 - But his flesh upon him shall have pain, and his soul within him shall mourn.

Job 33:19 - He is chastened also with pain upon his bed, and the multitude of his bones with strong [pain]:

PERSECUTION

2 Timothy 3:12 - Yea, and all that will live godly in Christ Jesus shall suffer persecution.

Matthew 5:44 - But I say unto you, Love your enemies, bless them that curse you, do good to them that hate you, and pray for them which despitefully use you, and persecute you;

1 Peter 3:17 - For [it is] better, if the will of God be so, that ye suffer for well doing, than for evil doing.

Matthew 5:10 - Blessed [are] they which are persecuted for righteousness' sake: for theirs is the kingdom of heaven.

Luke 6:22 - Blessed are ye, when men shall hate you, and when they shall separate you [from their company], and shall reproach [you], and cast out your name as evil, for the Son of man's sake.

POVERTY

2 Corinthians 8:9 - For ye know the grace of our Lord Jesus Christ, that, though he was rich, yet for your sakes he became poor, that ye through his poverty might be rich.

Proverbs 22:2 - The rich and poor meet together: the LORD [is] the maker of them all.

Proverbs 20:13 - Love not sleep, lest thou come to poverty; open thine eyes, [and] thou shalt be satisfied with bread.

Proverbs 31:9 Open thy mouth, judge righteously, and plead the cause of the poor and needy.

Luke 6:20 - And he lifted up his eyes on his disciples, and said, Blessed [be ye] poor: for yours is the kingdom of God.

Proverbs 28:11 - The rich man [is] wise in his own conceit; but the poor that hath understanding searcheth him out.

Proverbs 29:7 - The righteous considereth the cause of the poor: [but] the wicked regardeth not to know [it].

Proverbs 19:4 - Wealth maketh many friends; but the poor is separated from his neighbour.

Proverbs 22:7 - The rich ruleth over the poor, and the borrower [is] servant to the lender.

1 John 3:17 - But whoso hath this world's good, and seeth his brother have need, and shutteth up his bowels [of compassion] from him, how dwelleth the love of God in him?

PREJUDICE

Galatians 3:28 - There is neither Jew nor Greek, there is neither bond nor free, there is neither male nor female: for ye are all one in Christ Jesus.

Matthew 7:1 - Judge not, that ye be not judged.

Matthew 7:2 - For with what judgment ye judge, ye shall be judged: and with what measure ye mete, it shall be measured to you again.

Matthew 7:5 - Thou hypocrite, first cast out the beam out of thine own eye; and then shalt thou see clearly to case out the mote of thy brother's eye.

Acts 10:34 - Then Peter opened [his] mouth, and said, Of a truth I perceive that God is no respecter of persons:

John 17:11 - And now I am no more in the world, but these are in the world, and I come to thee. Holy Father, keep through thine own name those whom thou hast given me, that they may be one, as we [are].

Mark 12:31 - And the second [is] like, [namely] this, Thou shalt love thy neighbor as thyself. There is none other commandment greater than these.

PRESSURE

James 1:12 - Blessed [is] the man that endureth temptation: for when he is tried, he shall receive the crown of life, which the Lord hath promised to them that love him.

1 Corinthians 10:13 - There hath no temptation taken you but such as is common to man: but God [is] faithful, who will not suffer you to be tempted above that ye are able; but will with the temptation also make a way to escape, that ye may be able to bear [it].

2 Corinthians 10:3 - For though we walk in the flesh, we do not war after the flesh:

Proverbs 24:10 - [If] thou faint in the day of adversity, thy strength [is] small.

1 Peter 1:6 - Wherein ye greatly rejoice, though now for a season, if need be, ye are in heaviness through manifold temptations:

PRIDE

Proverbs 11:2 - [When] pride cometh, then cometh shame: but with the lowly [is] wisdom.

Proverbs 16:5 - Every one [that is] proud in heart [is] an abomination to the LORD: [though] hand [join] in hand, he shall not be unpunished.

Proverbs 29:23 - A man's pride shall bring him low: but honour shall uphold the humble in spirit.

Proverbs 16:18 - Pride [goeth] before destruction, and an haughty spirit before a fall.

James 4:6 - But he giveth more grace. Wherefore he saith, God resisteth the proud, but giveth grace unto the humble.

Proverbs 27:2 - Let another man praise thee, and not thine own mouth; a stranger, and not thine own lips.

Proverbs 26:12 - Seest thou a man wise in his own conceit? [there is] more hope of a fool than of him.

PROSTITUTION

Deuteronomy 23:18 - Thou shalt not bring the hire of a whore, or the price of a dog, into the house of the LORD thy God for any vow: for even both these [are] abomination unto the LORD thy God.

Proverbs 6:24 - To keep thee from the evil woman, from the flattery of the tongue of a strange woman.

Proverbs 6:25 - Lust not after her beauty in thine heart; neither let her take thee with her eyelids.

Proverbs 6:26 - For by means of a whorish woman [a man is brought] to a piece of bread: and the adulteress will hunt for the precious life.

Deuteronomy 23:17 - There shall be no whore of the daughters of Israel, nor a sodomite of the sons of Israel.

Leviticus 18:19 - Also thou shalt not approach unto a woman to uncover her nakedness, as long as she is put apart for her uncleanness.

PROVOKE

Numbers 14:11 - And the LORD said unto Moses, How long will this people provoke me? and how long will it be ere they believe me, for all the signs which I have shewed among them?

Numbers 14:23 - Surely they shall not see the land which I sware unto their fathers, neither shall any of them that provoked me see it:

Numbers 16:30 - But if the LORD make a new thing, and the earth open her mouth, and swallow them up, with all that appertain unto them, and they go down quick into the pit; then ye shall understand that these men have provoked the LORD.

Deuteronomy 9:18 - And I fell down before the LORD, as at the first, forty days and forty nights: I did neither eat bread, nor drink water, because of all your sins which ye sinned, in doing wickedly in the sight of the LORD, to provoke him to anger.

Deuteronomy 31:20 - For when I shall have brought them into the land which I sware unto their fathers, that floweth with milk and honey; and they shall have eaten and filled themselves, and waxen fat; then will they turn unto other gods, and serve them, and provoke me, and break my covenant.

Deuteronomy 32:16 - They provoked him to jealousy with strange gods, with abominations provoked they him to anger.

1 Kings 14:22 - And Judah did evil in the sight of the LORD, and they provoked him to jealousy with their sins which they had committed, above all that their fathers had done.

PUNISHMENT

Colossians 3:25 - But he that doeth wrong shall receive for the wrong which he hath done: and there is no respect of persons.

Genesis 9:6 - Whoso sheddeth man's blood, by man shall his blood be shed: for in the image of God made he man.

Exodus 21:17 - And he that curseth his father, or his mother, shall surely be put to death.

Matthew 25:41 - Then shall he say also unto them on the left hand, Depart from me, ye cursed, into everlasting fire, prepared for the devil and his angels:

Proverbs 11:21 - [Though] hand [join] in hand, the wicked shall not be unpunished: but the seed of the righteous shall be delivered.

Proverbs 22:3 - A prudent [man] foreseeth the evil, and hideth himself: but the simple pass on, and are punished.

RAGE

1 Corinthians 13:5 - Doth not behave itself unseemly, seeketh not her own, is not easily provoked, thinketh no evil;

Proverbs 14:17 - [He that is] soon angry dealeth foolishly: and a man of wicked devices is hated.

Proverbs 25:28 - He that [hath] no rule over his own spirit [is like] a city [that is] broken down, [and] without walls.

Proverbs 12:16 - A fool's wrath is presently known: but a prudent [man] covereth shame.

Proverbs 29:22 - An angry man stirreth up strife, and a furious man aboundeth in transgression.

Proverbs 20:1 - Wine [is] a mocker, strong drink [is] raging: and whosoever is deceived thereby is not wise.

Ephesians 4:27 – Neither give place to the devil.

REBELLIOUS

Proverbs 17:11 - An evil [man] seeketh only rebellion: therefore a cruel messenger shall be sent against him.

Psalms 68:6 - God setteth the solitary in families: he bringeth out those which are bound with chains: but the rebellious dwell in a dry [land].

Romans 13:2 - Whosoever therefore resisteth the power, resisteth the ordinance of God: and they that resist shall receive to themselves damnation.

Romans 13:3 - For rulers are not a terror to good works, but to the evil. Wilt thou then not be afraid of the power? do that which is good, and thou shalt have praise of the same:

Romans 13:7 - Render therefore to all their dues: tribute to whom tribute [is due]; custom to whom custom; fear to whom fear; honour to whom honour.

Exodus 20:3 - Thou shalt have no other gods before me.

REGRET

Philippians 3:13 - Brethren, I count not myself to have apprehended: but [this] one thing [I do], forgetting those things which are behind, and reaching forth unto those things which are before,

Isaiah 43:18 - Remember ye not the former things, neither consider the things of old.

Isaiah 43:19 - Behold, I will do a new thing; now it shall spring forth; shall ye not know it? I will even make a way in the wilderness, [and] rivers in the desert.

Isaiah 43:1 - But now thus saith the LORD that created thee, O Jacob, and he that formed thee, O Israel, Fear not: for I have redeemed thee, I have called [thee] by thy name; thou [art] mine.

Ecclesiastes 7:10 - Say not thou, What is [the cause] that the former days were better than these? for thou dost not enquire wisely concerning this.

Mark 11:24 - Therefore I say unto you, What things soever ye desire, when ye pray, believe that ye receive [them], and ye shall have [them].

Romans 8:28 - And we know that all things work together for good to them that love God, to them who are the called according to [his] purpose.

2 Timothy 4:7 - I have fought a good fight, I have finished [my] course, I have kept the faith:

REJECTION

Psalms 27:10 - When my father and my mother forsake me, then the LORD will take me up.

Psalms 94:14 - For the LORD will not cast off his people, neither will he forsake his inheritance.

Isaiah 53:3 - He is despised and rejected of men; a man of sorrows, and acquainted with grief: and we hid as it were [our] faces from him; he was despised, and we esteemed him not.

Luke 10:16 - He that heareth you heareth me; and he that despiseth you despiseth me; and he that despiseth me despiseth him that sent me.

John 1:11 - He came unto his own, and his own received him not.

Psalms 118:22 - The stone [which] the builders refused is become the head [stone] of the corner.

Romans 8:31 - What shall we then say to these things? If God [be] for us, who [can be] against us?

RESENTMENT

Mark 11:25 - And when ye stand praying, forgive, if ye have ought against any: that your Father also which is in heaven may forgive you your trespasses.

1 Peter 5:10 - But the God of all grace, who hath called us unto his eternal glory by Christ Jesus, after that ye have suffered a while, make you perfect, stablish, strengthen, settle [you].

James 5:16 - Confess [your] faults one to another, and pray one for another, that ye may be healed. The effectual fervent prayer of a righteous man availeth much.

Romans 12:2 - And be not conformed to this world: but be ye transformed by the renewing of your mind, that ye may prove what [is] that good, and acceptable, and perfect, will of God.

Romans 8:28 - And we know that all things work together for good to them that love God, to them who are the called according to [his] purpose.

REVENGE

Romans 12:19 - Dearly beloved, avenge not yourselves, but [rather] give place unto wrath: for it is written, Vengeance [is] mine; I will repay, saith the Lord.

Matthew 5:39 - But I say unto you, That ye resist not evil; but whosoever shall smite thee on thy right cheek, turn to them the other also.

1 Peter 3:9 - Not rendering evil for evil, or railing for railing: but contrariwise blessing; knowing that ye are thereunto called, that ye should inherit a blessing.

Proverbs 24:29 - Say not, I will do so to him as he hath done to me: I will render to the man according to his work.

Leviticus 19:18 - Thou shalt not avenge, nor bear any grudge against the children of thy people, but thou shalt love thy neighbour as thyself: I [am] the LORD.

1 Thessalonians 5:15 - See that none render evil for evil unto any [man]; but ever follow that which is good, both among yourselves, and to all [men].

Romans 13:4 - For he is the minister of God to thee for good. But if thou do that which is evil, be afraid; for he beareth not the sword in vain: for he is the minister of God, a revenger to [execute] wrath upon him that doeth evil.

SADNESS

James 5:13 - Is any among you afflicted? let him pray. Is any merry? let him sing psalms.

John 15:7 - If ye abide in me, and my words abide in you, ye shall ask what ye will, and it shall be done unto you.

Psalms 48:14 - For this God [is] our God for ever and ever: he will be our guide [even] unto death.

John 14:18 - I will not leave you comfortless: I will come to you.

John 10:29 - My Father, which gave [them] me, is greater than all; and no [man] is able to pluck [them] out of my Father's hand.

John 14:16 - And I will pray the Father, and he shall give you another Comforter, that he may abide with you for ever;

SATANIC

1 Peter 5:8 - Be sober, be vigilant; because your adversary the devil, as a roaring lion, walketh about, seeking whom he may devour:

1 John 3:8 - He that committeth sin is of the devil; for the devil sinneth from the beginning. For this purpose the Son of God was manifested, that he might destroy the works of the devil.

2 Corinthians 11:14 - And no marvel; for Satan himself is transformed into an angel of light.

John 8:44 - Ye are of [your] father the devil, and the lusts of your father ye will do. He was a murderer from the beginning, and abode not in the truth, because there is no truth in him. When he speaketh a lie, he speaketh of his own: for he is a liar, and the father of it.

James 4:7 - Submit yourselves therefore to God. Resist the devil, and he will flee from you.

Romans 16:20 - And the God of peace shall bruise Satan under your feet shortly. The grace of our Lord Jesus Christ [be] with you. Amen.

Revelation 12:9 - And the great dragon was cast out, that old serpent, called the Devil, and Satan, which deceiveth the whole world: he was cast out into the earth, and his angels were cast out with him.

Ephesians 6:11 - Put on the whole armour of God, that ye may be able to stand against the wiles of the devil.

Matthew 16:23 - But he turned, and said unto Peter, Get thee behind me, Satan: thou art an offence unto me: for thou savourest not the things that be of God, but those that be of men.

Ephesians 6:12 - For we wrestle not against flesh and blood, but against principalities, against powers, against the rulers of the darkness of this world, against spiritual wickedness in high [places].

Luke 10:18 - And he said unto them, I beheld Satan as lightning fall from heaven.

2 Corinthians 4:4 - In whom the god of this world hath blinded the minds of them which believe not, lest the light of the glorious gospel of Christ, who is the image of God, should shine unto them.

SELFISHNESS

1 John 3:17 - But whoso hath this world's good, and seeth his brother have need, and shutteth up his bowels [of compassion] from him, how dwelleth the love of God in him?

1 Corinthians 10:24 - Let no man seek his own, but every man another's [wealth].

Philippians 2:3- [Let] nothing [be done] through strife or vainglory; but in lowliness of mind let each esteem other better than themselves.

Philippians 2:21 - For all seek their own, not the things which are Jesus Christ's.

Romans 15:1 - We then that are strong ought to bear the infirmities of the weak, and not to please ourselves.

Luke 6:32 - For if ye love them which love you, what thank have ye? for sinners also love those that love them.

2 Timothy 2:4 - No man that warreth entangleth himself with the affairs of [this] life; that he may please him who hath chosen him to be a soldier.

SELF-RIGHTEOUSNESS

Titus 3:5 - Not by works of righteousness which we have done, but according to his mercy he saved us, by the washing of regeneration, and renewing of the Holy Ghost;

Galatians 2:16 - Knowing that a man is not justified by the works of the law, but by the faith of Jesus Christ, even we have believed in Jesus Christ, that we might be justified by the faith of Christ, and not by the works of the law: for by the works of the law shall no flesh be justified.

Luke 10:27 - And he answering said, Thou shalt love the Lord thy God with all thy heart, and with all thy soul, and with all thy strength, and with all thy mind; and thy neighbour as thyself.

Romans 10:3 - For they being ignorant of God's righteousness, and going about to establish their own righteousness, have not submitted themselves unto the righteousness of God.

Mark 12:31 - And the second [is] like, [namely] this, Thou shalt love thy neighbour as thyself. There is none other commandment greater than these.

John 14:15 - If ye love me, keep my commandments.

1 John 1:9 - If we confess our sins, he is faithful and just to forgive us [our] sins, and to cleanse us from all unrighteousness.

SHAME

Isaiah 50:7 - For the Lord GOD will help me; therefore, shall I not be confounded: therefore have I set my face like a flint, and I know that I shall not be ashamed.

Hebrews 12:2 - Looking unto Jesus the author and finisher of [our] faith; who for the joy that was set before him endured the cross, despising the shame, and is set down at the right hand of the throne of God.

Psalms 34:5 - They looked unto him, and were lightened: and their faces were not ashamed.

Romans 10:11 - For the scripture saith, Whosoever believeth on him shall not be ashamed.

Psalms 31:17 - Let me not be ashamed, O LORD; for I have called upon thee: let the wicked be ashamed, [and] let them be silent in the grave.

Psalms 3:3 - But thou, O LORD, [art] a shield for me; my glory, and the lifter up of mine head.

Mark 8:38 - Whosoever therefore shall be ashamed of me and of my words in this adulterous and sinful generation; of him also shall the Son of man be ashamed, when he cometh in the glory of his Father with the holy angels.

Psalms 25:1 - Unto thee, O LORD, do I lift up my soul.

SICKNESS

3 John 1:2 - Beloved, I wish above all things that thou mayest prosper and be in health, even as thy soul prospereth.

James 5:14 - Is any sick among you? let him call for the elders of the church; and let them pray over him, anointing him with oil in the name of the Lord:

James 5:15 - And the prayer of faith shall save the sick, and the Lord shall raise him up; and if he have committed sins, they shall be forgiven him.

1 Peter 2:24 - Who his own self bare our sins in his own body on the tree, that we, being dead to sins, should live unto righteousness: by whose stripes ye were healed.

Luke 9:1 - Then he called his twelve disciples together, and gave them power and authority over all devils, and to cure diseases.

Isaiah 53:5 - But he [was] wounded for our transgressions, [he was] bruised for our iniquities: the chastisement of our peace [was] upon him; and with his stripes we are healed.

Luke 10:9 - And heal the sick that are therein, and say unto them, The kingdom of God is come nigh unto you.

SLANDER

Matthew 12:36 - But I say unto you, That every idle word that men shall speak, they shall give account thereof in the day of judgment.

Psalms 101:5 - Whoso privily slandereth his neighbour, him will I cut off: him that hath an high look and a proud heart will not I suffer.

1 Peter 3:16 - Having a good conscience; that, whereas they speak evil of you, as of evildoers, they may be ashamed that falsely accuse your good conversation in Christ.

Proverbs 10:18 - He that hideth hatred [with] lying lips, and he that uttereth a slander, [is] a fool.

Proverbs 11:9 - An hypocrite with [his] mouth destroyeth his neighbour: but through knowledge shall the just be delivered.

Psalms 109:3 - They compassed me about also with words of hatred; and fought against me without a cause.

SLOTH

Proverbs 12:24 - The hand of the diligent shall bear rule: but the slothful shall be under tribute.

Proverbs 15:19 - The way of the slothful [man is] as an hedge of thorns: but the way of the righteous [is] made plain.

Proverbs 21:25 - The desire of the slothful killeth him; for his hands refuse to labour.

Proverbs 24:30 - I went by the field of the slothful, and by the vineyard of the man void of understanding;

Ecclesiastes 10:18 - By much slothfulness the building decayeth; and through idleness of the hands the house droppeth through.

Proverbs 6:6 - Go to the ant, thou sluggard; consider her ways, and be wise:

Proverbs 6:8 - Provideth her meat in the summer, [and] gathereth her food in the harvest.

Matthew 25:26 - His lord answered and said unto him, [Thou] wicked and slothful servant, thou knewest that I reap where I sowed not, and gather where I have not strawed:

Romans 12:11 - Not slothful in business; fervent in spirit; serving the Lord;

SORROW

Revelation 21:4 - And God shall wipe away all tears from their eyes; and there shall be no more death, neither sorrow, nor crying, neither shall there be any more pain: for the former things are passed away.

Psalms 30:5 - For his anger [endureth but] a moment; in his favour [is] life: weeping may endure for a night, but joy [cometh] in the morning.

2 Corinthians 7:10 - For godly sorrow worketh repentance to salvation not to be repented of: but the sorrow of the world worketh death.

Proverbs 10:22 - The blessing of the LORD, it maketh rich, and he addeth no sorrow with it.

John 16:22 - And ye now therefore have sorrow: but I will see you again, and your heart shall rejoice, and your joy no man taketh from you.

STEAL

Ephesians 4:28 - Let him that stole steal no more: but rather let him labour, working with [his] hands the thing which is good, that he may have to give to him that needeth.

Exodus 20:15 - Thou shalt not steal.

Leviticus 19:11 - Ye shall not steal, neither deal falsely, neither lie one to another.

Jeremiah 7:11 – Is this house, which is called by my name, become a den of robbers in your eyes? Behold, even I have seen [it], saith the LORD.

Psalms 62:10 - Trust not in oppression, and become not vain in robbery: if riches increase, set not your heart [upon them].

John 10:10 - The thief cometh not, but for to steal, and to kill, and to destroy: I am come that they might have life, and that they might have [it] more abundantly.

STRESS

John 14:27 - Peace I leave with you, my peace I give unto you: not as the world giveth, give I unto you. Let not your heart be troubled, neither let it be afraid.

John 16:33 - These things I have spoken unto you, that in me ye might have peace. In the world ye shall have tribulation: but be of good cheer; I have overcome the world.

Romans 8:31 - What shall we then say to these things? If God [be] for us, who [can be] against us?

Philippians 4:13 - I can do all things through Christ which strengtheneth me.

Psalms 34:17 - [The righteous] cry, and the LORD heareth, and delivereth them out of all their troubles.

Psalms 34:19 – Many [are] the afflictions of the righteous: but the LORD delivereth him out of them all.

STRIFE

2 Timothy 2:23 - But foolish and unlearned questions avoid, knowing that they do gender strifes.

Proverbs 20:3 - [It is] an honour for a man to cease from strife: but every fool will be meddling.

Proverbs 29:22 - An angry man stirreth up strife, and a furious man aboundeth in transgression.

Proverbs 28:25 - He that is of a proud heart stirreth up strife: but he that putteth his trust in the LORD shall be made fat.

James 3:16 - For where envying and strife [is], there [is] confusion and every evil work.

Proverbs 22:10 - Cast out the scorner, and contention shall go out; yea, strife and reproach shall cease.

SUFFER

1 Peter 5:10 - But the God of all grace, who hath called us unto his eternal glory by Christ Jesus, after that ye have suffered a while, make you perfect, stablish, strengthen, settle [you].

Romans 8:18 - For I reckon that the sufferings of this present time [are] not worthy [to be compared] with the glory which shall be revealed in us.

1 Peter 4:13 - But rejoice, inasmuch as ye are partakers of Christ's sufferings; that, when his glory shall be revealed, ye may be glad also with exceeding joy.

1 Peter 4:15 - But let none of you suffer as a murderer, or [as] a thief, or [as] an evildoer, or as a busybody in other men's matters.

1 Peter 4:16 - Yet if [any man suffer] as a Christian, let him not be ashamed; but let him glorify God on this behalf.

1 Peter 4:19 Wherefore let them that suffer according to the will of God commit the keeping of their souls [to him] in well doing, as unto a faithful Creator.

Isaiah 43:2 - When thou passest through the waters, I [will be] with thee; and through the rivers, they shall not overflow thee: when thou walkest through the fire, thou shalt not be burned; neither shall the flame kindle upon thee.

2 Timothy 3:12 - Yea, and all that will live godly in Christ Jesus shall suffer persecution.

SUICIDE

1 Corinthians 3:16 - Know ye not that ye are the temple of God, and [that] the Spirit of God dwelleth in you?

1 Corinthians 3:17 - If any man defile the temple of God, him shall God destroy; for the temple of God is holy, which [temple] ye are.

Ecclesiastes 7:17 - Be not over much wicked, neither be thou foolish: why shouldest thou die before thy time?

Psalms 34:17 - [The righteous] cry, and the LORD heareth, and delivereth them out of all their troubles.

Psalms 34:19 - Many [are] the afflictions of the righteous: but the LORD delivereth him out of them all.

1 Corinthians 6:19 - What? know ye not that your body is the temple of the Holy Ghost [which

is] in you, which ye have of God, and ye are not your own?

1 Corinthians 6:20 - For ye are bought with a price: therefore glorify God in your body, and in your spirit, which are God's.

Proverbs 3:6 - In all thy ways acknowledge him, and he shall direct thy paths.

Psalms 13:3 - Consider [and] hear me, O LORD my God: lighten mine eyes, lest I sleep the [sleep of] death;

Deuteronomy 30:19 - I call heaven and earth to record this day against you, [that] I have set before you life and death, blessing and cursing: therefore choose life, that both thou and thy seed may live:

John 10:28 - And I give unto them eternal life; and they shall never perish, neither shall any [man] pluck them out of my hand.

SWEAR

James 5:12 - But above all things, my brethren, swear not, neither by heaven, neither by the earth, neither by any other oath: but let your yea be yea; and [your] nay, nay; lest ye fall into condemnation.

Matthew 5:33 - Again, ye have heard that it hath been said by them of old time, Thou shalt not forswear thyself, but shalt perform unto the Lord thine oaths:

Matthew 5:34 - But I say unto you, Swear not at all; neither by heaven; for it is God's throne:

Matthew 5:35 - Nor by the earth; for it is his footstool: neither by Jerusalem; for it is the city of the great King.

Matthew 5:36 - Neither shalt thou swear by thy head, because thou canst not make one hair white or black.

Matthew 12:36 - But I say unto you, That every idle word that men shall speak, they shall give account thereof in the day of judgment.

Exodus 20:7 - Thou shalt not take the name of the LORD thy God in vain; for the LORD will not hold him guiltless that taketh his name in vain.

Hosea 4:2 - By swearing, and lying, and killing, and stealing, and committing adultery, they break out, and blood toucheth blood.

TEMPTATION

1 Corinthians 10:13 - There hath no temptation taken you but such as is common to man: but God [is] faithful, who will not suffer you to be tempted above that ye are able; but will with the temptation also make a way to escape, that ye may be able to bear [it].

Matthew 26:41 - Watch and pray, that ye enter not into temptation: the spirit indeed [is] willing, but the flesh [is] weak.

James 4:7 - Submit yourselves therefore to God. Resist the devil, and he will flee from you.

Hebrews 2:18 - For in that he himself hath suffered being tempted, he is able to succour them that are tempted.

Matthew 4:1 - Then was Jesus led up of the Spirit into the wilderness to be tempted of the devil.

James 1:2 - My brethren, count it all joy when ye fall into divers temptations;

TERRORISM

Matthew 24:9 - Then shall they deliver you up to be afflicted, and shall kill you: and ye shall be hated of all nations for my name's sake.

Matthew 24:6 - And ye shall hear of wars and rumours of wars: see that ye be not troubled: for all [these things] must come to pass, but the end is not yet.

Psalms 34:14 - Depart from evil, and do good; seek peace, and pursue it.

Psalms 10:17 - LORD, thou hast heard the desire of the humble: thou wilt prepare their heart, thou wilt cause thine ear to hear:

Romans 13:1 - Let every soul be subject unto the higher powers. For there is no power but of God: the powers that be are ordained of God.

Luke 12:4 - And I say unto you my friends, Be not afraid of them that kill the body, and after that have no more that they can do.

THIEVES

Ephesians 4:28 - Let him that stole steal no more: but rather let him labour, working with [his] hands the thing which is good, that he may have to give to him that needeth.

John 10:10 - The thief cometh not, but for to steal, and to kill, and to destroy: I am come that they might have life, and that they might have [it] more abundantly.

1 John 2:4 - He that saith, I know him, and keepeth not his commandments, is a liar, and the truth is not in him.

Exodus 22:1 - If a man shall steal an ox, or a sheep, and kill it, or sell it; he shall restore five oxen for an ox, and four sheep for a sheep.

Exodus 22:2 - If a thief be found breaking up, and be smitten that he die, [there shall] no blood [be shed] for him.

THREATS

Isaiah 54:17 - No weapon that is formed against thee shall prosper; and every tongue [that] shall rise against thee in judgment thou shalt condemn. This [is] the heritage of the servants of the LORD, and their righteousness [is] of me, saith the LORD.

Matthew 26:52 - Then said Jesus unto him, Put up again thy sword into his place: for all they that take the sword shall perish with the sword.

Matthew 5:38 - Ye have heard that it hath been said, An eye for an eye, and a tooth for a tooth:

Proverbs 29:11 - A fool uttereth all his mind: but a wise [man] keepeth it in till afterwards.

Romans 13:4 - For he is the minister of God to thee for good. But if thou do that which is evil, be afraid; for he beareth not the sword in vain: for he is the minister of God, a revenger to [execute] wrath upon him that doeth evil.

Psalms 46:1 - (To the chief Musician for the sons of Korah, A Song upon Alamoth.) God [is] our refuge and strength, a very present help in trouble.

TORMENT

Matthew 4:24 - And his fame went throughout all Syria: and they brought unto him all sick people that were taken with divers diseases and torments, and those which were possessed with devils, and those which were lunatic, and those that had the palsy; and he healed them.

Luke 8:28 - When he saw Jesus, he cried out, and fell down before him, and with a loud voice said, What have I to do with thee, Jesus, thou Son of God most high? I beseech thee, torment me not.

Luke 16:23 - And in hell he lift up his eyes, being in torment, and seeth Abraham afar off, and Lazarus in his bosom.

Luke 16:24 - And he cried and said, Father Abraham, have mercy on me, and send Lazarus, that he may dip the tip of his finger in water, and cool my tongue; for I am tormented in this flame.

Luke 16:25 - But Abraham said, Son, remember that thou in thy lifetime receivedst thy good things, and likewise Lazarus evil things: but now he is comforted, and thou art tormented.

Revelation 14:11 - And the smoke of their torment ascendeth up for ever and ever: and they have no rest day nor night, who worship the beast and his image, and whosoever receiveth the mark of his name.

Revelation 20:10 - And the devil that deceived them was cast into the lake of fire and brimstone, where the beast and the false prophet are, and shall be tormented day and night for ever and ever.

TRANSGRESSION

1 Chronicles 10:13 - So Saul died for his transgression which he committed against the LORD, even against the word of the LORD, which he kept not, and also for asking counsel of one that had a familiar spirit, to enquire of it;

Job 33:9 - I am clean without transgression, I am innocent; neither is there iniquity in me.

Job 36:9 - Then he sheweth them their work, and their transgression that they have exceeded.

Psalms 25:7 - Remember not the sins of my youth, nor my transgression: according to thy mercy remember thou me for thy goodness' sake, O LORD.

Psalms 32:5 - I acknowledged my sin unto thee, and mine iniquity have I not hid. I said, I will confess my transgression unto the LORD; and thou forgavest the iniquity of my sin. Selah.

TRESPASS

Matthew 18:15 - Moreover if thy brother shall trespass against thee, go and tell him his fault between thee and him alone: if he shall hear thee, thou hast gained thy brother.

Luke 17:4 - And if he trespass against thee seven times in a day, and seven times in a day turn again to thee, saying, I repent; thou shalt forgive him.

1 Samuel 25:28 - I pray thee, forgive the trespass of thine handmaid: for the LORD will certainly make my lord a sure house; because my lord fighteth the battles of the LORD, and evil hath not been found in thee [all] thy days.

Matthew 6:15 – But if ye forgive not men their trespasses, nether will your Father forgive your trespasses.

UNFAITHFUL

1 Corinthians 7:2 - Nevertheless, [to avoid] fornication, let every man have his own wife, and let every woman have her own husband.

1 Corinthians 7:3 - Let the husband render unto the wife due benevolence: and likewise also the wife unto the husband.

1 Corinthians 7:4 - The wife hath not power of her own body, but the husband: and likewise also the husband hath not power of his own body, but the wife.

Hebrews 13:4 - Marriage [is] honourable in all, and the bed undefiled: but whoremongers and adulterers God will judge.

Matthew 5:28 – But I say unto you, That whosoever looketh on a woman to lust after he hath committed adultery with her already in his heart.

Ephesians 5:28 - So ought men to love their wives as their own bodies. He that loveth his wife loveth himself.

UGLY

Isaiah 64:8 - But now, O LORD, thou [art] our father; we [are] the clay, and thou our potter; and we all [are] the work of thy hand.

Isaiah 62:3 - Thou shalt also be a crown of glory in the hand of the LORD, and a royal diadem in the hand of thy God.

Genesis 1:31 - And God saw everything that he had made, and, behold, [it was] very good. And the evening and the morning were the sixth day.

Job 31:15 - Did not he that made me in the womb make him? and did not one fashion us in the womb.

1 Samuel 16:7 - But the LORD said unto Samuel, Look not on his countenance, or on the height of his stature; because I have refused him: for [the LORD seeth] not as man seeth; for man looketh on the outward appearance, but the LORD looketh on the heart.

1 Peter 3:3 - Whose adorning let it not be that outward [adorning] of plaiting the hair, and of wearing of gold, or of putting on of apparel;

1 Peter 3:4 - But [let it be] the hidden man of the heart, in that which is not corruptible, [even the ornament] of a meek and quiet spirit, which is in the sight of God of great price.

Hebrews 10:35 - Cast not away therefore your confidence, which hath great recompence of reward.

UNBELIEF

Mark 9:23- - Jesus said unto him, If thou canst believe, all things [are] possible to him that believeth.

John 3:18 - He that believeth on him is not condemned: but he that believeth not is condemned already, because he hath not believed in the name of the only begotten Son of God.

John 12:48 - He that rejecteth me, and receiveth not my words, hath one that judgeth him: the word that I have spoken, the same shall judge him in the last day.

2 Timothy 3:5 - Having a form of godliness, but denying the power thereof: from such turn away.

Isaiah 66:2 - For all those [things] hath mine hand made, and all those [things] have been, saith the LORD: but to this [man] will I look, [even] to [him that is] poor and of a contrite spirit, and trembleth at my word.

Matthew 17:20 - And Jesus said unto them, Because of your unbelief: for verily I say unto you, If ye have faith as a grain of mustard seed, ye shall say unto this mountain, Remove hence to yonder place; and it shall remove; and nothing shall be impossible unto you.

2 Corinthians 6:14 - Be ye not unequally yoked together with unbelievers: for what fellowship hath righteousness with unrighteousness? and what communion hath light with darkness?

Romans 10:4 - For Christ [is] the end of the law for righteousness to everyone that believeth.

UNFORGIVENESS

Matthew 6:14 - For if ye forgive men their trespasses, your heavenly Father will also forgive you:

Ephesians 4:32 - And be ye kind one to another, tenderhearted, forgiving one another, even as God for Christ's sake hath forgiven you.

Hebrews 12:14 - Follow peace with all [men], and holiness, without which no man shall see the Lord:

Colossians 3:13 - Forbearing one another, and forgiving one another, if any man have a quarrel against any: even as Christ forgave you, so also [do] ye.

2 Corinthians 2:10 - To whom ye forgive anything, I [forgive] also: for if I forgave anything, to whom I forgave [it], for your sakes [forgave I it] in the person of Christ;

Matthew 6:12 - And forgive us our debts, as we forgive our debtors.

UNGODLY

Psalms 1:4 - The ungodly are not so: but are like the chaff which the wind driveth away.

Psalms 1:5 - Therefore the ungodly shall not stand in the judgment, nor sinners in the congregation of the righteous.

Psalms 1:6 - For the LORD knoweth the way of the righteous: but the way of the ungodly shall perish.

Psalms 3:7 - Arise, O LORD; save me, O my God: for thou hast smitten all mine enemies upon the cheek bone; thou hast broken the teeth of the ungodly.

Proverbs 16:27 - An ungodly man diggeth up evil: and in his lips there is as a burning fire.

Romans 5:6 - For when we were yet without strength, in due time Christ died for the ungodly.

2 Peter 3:7 - But the heavens and the earth, which are now, by the same word are kept in store, reserved unto fire against the day of judgment and perdition of ungodly men.

Jude 1:4 - For there are certain men crept in unawares, who were before of old ordained to this condemnation, ungodly men, turning the grace of our God into lasciviousness, and denying the only Lord God, and our Lord Jesus Christ.

UNRIGHTEOUSNESS

Leviticus 19:15 - Ye shall do no unrighteousness in judgment: thou shalt not respect the person of the poor, nor honour the person of the mighty: but in righteousness shalt thou judge thy neighbour.

Leviticus 19:35 - Ye shall do no unrighteousness in judgment, in meteyard, in weight, or in measure.

Psalms 92:15 - To shew that the LORD is upright: he is my rock, and there is no unrighteousness in him.

Romans 6:13 - Neither yield ye your members as instruments of unrighteousness unto sin: but yield yourselves unto God, as those that are alive from the dead, and your members as instruments of righteousness unto God.

2 Corinthians 6:14 - Be ye not unequally yoked together with unbelievers: for what fellowship

hath righteousness with unrighteousness? and what communion hath light with darkness?

2 Thessalonians 2:12 - That they all might be damned who believed not the truth, but had pleasure in unrighteousness.

Hebrews 8:12 - For I will be merciful to their unrighteousness, and their sins and their iniquities will I remember no more.

VANITY

Psalms 119:37 - Turn away mine eyes from beholding vanity; [and] quicken thou me in thy way.

1 Samuel 16:7 - But the LORD said unto Samuel, Look not on his countenance, or on the height of his stature; because I have refused him: for [the LORD seeth] not as man seeth; for man looketh on the outward appearance, but the LORD looketh on the heart.

Ecclesiastes 5:10 - He that loveth silver shall not be satisfied with silver; nor he that loveth abundance with increase: this [is] also vanity.

1 Timothy 4:8 - For bodily exercise profiteth little: but godliness is profitable unto all things, having promise of the life that now is, and of that which is to come.

Ecclesiastes 2:11 - Then I looked on all the works that my hands had wrought, and on the labour that I had laboured to do: and, behold, all [was] vanity and vexation of spirit, and [there was] no profit under the sun.

Ecclesiastes 1:2 - Vanity of vanities, saith the Preacher, vanity of vanities; all [is] vanity.

VIOLENCE

Matthew 26:52 - Then said Jesus unto him, Put up again thy sword into his place: for all they that take the sword shall perish with the sword.

Isaiah 60:18 - Violence shall no more be heard in thy land, wasting nor destruction within thy borders; but thou shalt call thy walls Salvation, and thy gates Praise.

Genesis 9:5 - And surely your blood of your lives will I require; at the hand of every beast will I require it, and at the hand of man; at the hand of every man's brother will I require the life of man.

Titus 3:2 - To speak evil of no man, to be no brawlers, [but] gentle, shewing all meekness unto all men.

Psalms 144:1 - Blessed [be] the LORD my strength, which teacheth my hands to war, [and] my fingers to fight:

Psalms 55:15 - Let death seize upon them, [and] let them go down quick into hell: for wickedness [is] in their dwellings, [and] among them.

Romans 14:10 - But why dost thou judge thy brother? or why dost thou set at nought thy brother? for we shall all stand before the judgment seat of Christ.

VOO DOO

Revelation 22:15 – Four without are dogs, and sorcerers, and whoremongers, and murderers, and idolaters, and whomever loveth and maket a lie.

Acts 16:16 - And it came to pass, as we went to prayer, a certain damsel possessed with a spirit of divination met us, which brought her masters much gain by soothsaying:

Exodus 22:18 - Thou shalt not suffer a witch to live.

1 John 4:1 - Beloved, believe not every spirit, but try the spirits whether they are of God: because many false prophets are gone out into the world.

Deuteronomy 18:11 - Or a charmer, or a consulter with familiar spirits, or a wizard, or a necromancer.

WHORE

Deuteronomy 23:17 - There shall be no whore of the daughters of Israel, nor a sodomite of the sons of Israel.

Hebrews 13:4 - Marriage [is] honourable in all, and the bed undefiled: but whoremongers and adulterers God will judge.

Jeremiah 3:1 - They say, If a man put away his wife, and she go from him, and become another man's, shall he return unto her again? shall not that land be greatly polluted? but thou hast played the harlot with many lovers; yet return again to me, saith the LORD.

Revelation 17:4 - And the woman was arrayed in purple and scarlet colour, and decked with gold and precious stones and pearls, having a golden cup in her hand full of abominations and filthiness of her fornication:

Revelation 17:1 - And there came one of the seven angels which had the seven vials, and talked with me, saying unto me, Come hither; I will shew unto thee the judgment of the great whore that sitteth upon many waters:

WICKED

Proverbs 24:19 - Fret not thyself because of evil [men], neither be thou envious at the wicked;

Proverbs 10:24 - The fear of the wicked, it shall come upon him: but the desire of the righteous shall be granted.

Psalms 141:10 - Let the wicked fall into their own nets, whilst that I withal escape.

Proverbs 25:26 - A righteous man falling down before the wicked [is as] a troubled fountain, and a corrupt spring.

Revelation 21:8 - But the fearful, and unbelieving, and the abominable, and murderers, and whoremongers, and sorcerers, and idolaters, and all liars, shall have their part in the lake which burneth with fire and brimstone: which is the second death.

Ecclesiastes 5:1 - Keep thy foot when thou goest to the house of God, and be more ready to hear, than to give the sacrifice of fools: for they consider not that they do evil.

WITCHCRAFT

Leviticus 20:27 - A man also or woman that hath a familiar spirit, or that is a wizard, shall surely be put to death: they shall stone them with stones: their blood [shall be] upon them.

Deuteronomy 18:10 - There shall not be found among you [any one] that maketh his son or his daughter to pass through the fire, [or] that useth divination, [or] an observer of times, or an enchanter, or a witch,

Galatians 5:20 - Idolatry, witchcraft, hatred, variance, emulations, wrath, strife, seditions, heresies,

2 Chronicles 33:6 - And he caused his children to pass through the fire in the valley of the son of Hinnom: also he observed times, and used enchantments, and used witchcraft, and dealt with a familiar spirit, and with wizards: he wrought much evil in the sight of the LORD, to provoke him to anger.

1 Samuel 15:23 - For rebellion [is as] the sin of witchcraft, and stubbornness [is as] iniquity and idolatry. Because thou hast rejected the word of the LORD, he hath also rejected thee from [being] king.

Micah 5:12 - And I will cut off witchcrafts out of thine hand; and thou shalt have no [more] soothsayers:

WOE

Ecclesiastes 4:10 - For if they fall, the one will lift up his fellow: but woe to him [that is] alone when he falleth; for [he hath] not another to help him up.

Isaiah 3:11 - Woe unto the wicked! [it shall be] ill [with him]: for the reward of his hands shall be given him.

Isaiah 5:8 - Woe unto them that join house to house, [that] lay field to field, till [there be] no place, that they may be placed alone in the midst of the earth!

Isaiah 5:20 - Woe unto them that call evil good, and good evil; that put darkness for light, and light for darkness; that put bitter for sweet, and sweet for bitter!

Isaiah 5:21 - Woe unto [them that are] wise in their own eyes, and prudent in their own sight!

Isaiah 6:5 - Then said I, Woe [is] me! for I am undone; because I [am] a man of unclean lips, and I dwell in the midst of a people of unclean lips: for mine eyes have seen the King, the LORD of hosts.

Isaiah 29:15 - Woe unto them that seek deep to hide their counsel from the LORD, and their works are in the dark, and they say, Who seeth us? and who knoweth us?

WORRY

Philippians 4:6 - Be careful for nothing; but in everything by prayer and supplication with thanksgiving let your requests be made known unto God.

Philippians 4:7 – And the peace of God, which passeth all understanding, shall keep your hearts and minds through Christ Jesus.

Matthew 6:25 - Therefore I say unto you, Take no thought for your life, what ye shall eat, or what ye shall drink; nor yet for your body, what ye shall put on. Is not the life more than meat, and the body than raiment?

1 Peter 5:7 - Casting all your care upon him; for he careth for you.

Matthew 6:33 - But seek ye first the kingdom of God, and his righteousness; and all these things shall be added unto you.

Philippians 4:13 - I can do all things through Christ which strengtheneth me.

Matthew 11:28 - Come unto me, all [ye] that labour and are heavy laden, and I will give you rest.

Matthew 6:27 - Which of you by taking thought can add one cubit unto his stature?

John 14:27 - Peace I leave with you, my peace I give unto you: not as the world giveth, give I unto you. Let not your heart be troubled, neither let it be afraid.

Philippians 4:19 - But my God shall supply all your need according to his riches in glory by Christ Jesus.

WORTHLESSNESS

Philippians 4:7 - And the peace of God, which passeth all understanding, shall keep your hearts and minds through Christ Jesus.

Philippians 1:6 - Being confident of this very thing, that he which hath begun a good work in you will perform [it] until the day of Jesus Christ:

Romans 8:18 - For I reckon that the sufferings of this present time [are] not worthy [to be compared] with the glory which shall be revealed in us.

Romans 8:26 - Likewise the Spirit also helpeth our infirmities: for we know not what we should pray for as we ought: but the Spirit itself maketh intercession for us with groanings which cannot be uttered.

Ephesians 2:10 - For we are his workmanship, created in Christ Jesus unto good works, which

God hath before ordained that we should walk in them.

1 John 1:9 - If we confess our sins, he is faithful and just to forgive us [our] sins, and to cleanse us from all unrighteousness.

ADDITIONAL SCRIPTURES - OF ROBES, TURBAN, FILTHY RAGS, JEWELS, FINE LINEN, KING AND LORD.

Revelation 7:14—And I said unto him, Sir, thou knowest. And he said to me, These are they which came out of great tribulation, and have washed their robes, and made them white in the blood of the Lamb.
(KJV)

Job 29:14 —Everything I did was honest. Righteousness covered me like a robe, and I wore justice like a turban. (NLT)

Isaiah 64:6—We are all infected and impure with sin. When we display our righteous deeds, they are nothing but filthy rags. Like autumn leaves, we wither and fall, and our sins sweep us away like the wind. (NLT)

Isaiah 61:10—I am overwhelmed with joy in the Lord my God! For He has dressed me with the clothing of salvation and draped me in a robe of righteousness. I am like a bridegroom dressed for his wedding or a bride with her jewels. (NLT)

Revelation 19:8—She has been given the finest of pure white linen to wear." For the fine linen represents the good deeds of God's holy people. (NLT)

Revelation 19:16— On his robe and at his thigh he has this name written: king of kings and lord of lords. (NLT)

About the Author

Janice Marie Horne Brown was born in Wilson, North Carolina. She lived most of her childhood in Elm City, North Carolina. During her last year in high school, she met and married her high school sweetheart Prentis Brown Jr, a Sergeant in the United States Air Force. After graduating from high school, she moved to Fayetteville, North Carolina. She is blessed with a wonderful son, Prentis Brown III and later a beautiful daughter-in-law Victoria Boykins-Brown who has a very sweet spirit and a special place in her heart. Janice is very close to her family whom she considers very special and the second most important to her. In 1987, she became a born again Christian and she loves the Lord her Savior Jesus Christ wholeheartedly. She is strongly convinced that God is the first and the center of her life!

Janice attended and graduated from several Colleges throughout her world travel alongside her husband with the military. She obtained several Diplomas and Associate Degrees in which she majored in Early Childhood and Education at Northwest Florida State College, Niceville, Fl., California State University, Northridge, California, Central Texas Colleges, Killeen, Texas.

Janice has a great love for God's word, so she became a steward of His word. She received several degrees majoring in Theology and obtaining her Associates, Bachelor, and Master of Theology while studying at Christian Life School of Theology Global and Rivers School of Ministry, Fayetteville, North Carolina. Today she is currently pursuing her Doctor of Sacred Studies and Doctor of Theology. She is one of God's servant, ready, willing and able - a soldier in God's army to preach His word whenever called upon. She is also active in the Children Ministries, Ministerial Care Team, Prayer Team-Prayer Warrior (Intercessors), very active in the Women Fellowship Ministry, ministering diligently with monthly family prayer meetings, church community and the surrounding areas.

Janice career has expanded over the years of working for the government. Throughout her world travels, she has worked with the United States Air Force and the United States Army. She has traveled to many places such as Misawa Air Base, Japan, Kadena Air Force Base Japan, Tokyo Japan, Guam, Alaska, California, Hawaii, St Louis, Eglin Air Base Florida, Minnesota, Minneapolis, Charleston Air Base South Carolina, Georgia, Louisiana, Virginia, Baltimore, Washington DC, North Dakota, Mississippi, Pennsylvania, Michigan, Alabama, Ohio and North Carolina.

As a results she became very experienced a specialist with a demonstrated history of working in the Early Childhood and Education management industry, Skilled as an Overseer of multiple Child Care and Youth Facilities as well as in Classroom Management, Youth Director, Youth Counselor, School Age Coordinator, Child Development Director, Playground Specialist, Trainer & Curriculum Development, Typing Instructor, Teacher, Presenter for many Educational Workshops, Conferences and Public Speaking. In 2003, she became an Owner and

Operator of her own business, Little Treasure Day Care.

She realized that God blessed her with a special talent, a burden heart for working with children. He blessed her with a gifted mind of creative writing. She began to write, develop curriculums, creating and directing plays. God also blessed her with gifted hands, where she became very skilled at developing stage props and creating costumes for children. She was so elated to see how much the children were drawn to learning through theater arts. She is an Advocate for children. Her long-term goal is to open a Theater Arts and Mentoring Academy School.

She looks forward to sharing with children and young adults the wonders of God's word, by giving them a platform to perform their best while bringing the pages of the Bible to life! She feels that high-quality and programs will teach children and young adults about self-help skills and to inspire them to become a positive member of their community and a productive member of our society.

Early Childhood and Education became her passion. She believes that we live in a society where everyone is on the go. She has seen too many of our children falling through the cracks, going without, unnoticed, unloved, unheard, gone astray, no sense of direction, uncared for and poor life changing choices. She has challenged every child care professional in this field, to find a way to make a different in a child's life and not let it always be about the paycheck. She feels that we all know that in this field the riches will come only in the bounty of love that we bestowed upon the children.

She feels that patience --- God's gift of the fruit of the spirit --- is a virtue and a necessity, especially when working with God's little children. She aspired to make children's lives happier and more meaningful.

Her mission is to provide developmentally appropriate programs to foster the development of children. She believes in the value and uniqueness of each child and she strives to meet the learning styles of each child. She believes that young children need to be actively involved in learning through play and have the opportunities to explore, experience and succeed. She always provided a warm, caring, nurturing environment for the strong imagination, creativity and life skills. She believes we should nurture each in developing a positive self-image, knowing he/she are accepted as an individual, while maintaining a sense of belonging.

She believes that children should be able to have maximum opportunities to discover, explore and problem solve, in or to make independent choices within a developmentally appropriate and inclusive environment. She believes that each child should experience a high-quality program and a safe environment to ensure their right to learn. She feels that it is important to honor each child and their family's cultural, linguistic, racial and socioeconomic diversity in order to increase the self-awareness of everyone.

God blessed Janice to Long display her talent and to share her love for children throughout her world travel and the United States. While deployed at Misawa Air Force Base Japan, she spearheaded and expanded several programs within the American and Japanese community in accordance with strategic and operating plans that ensured high quality programs and established new program activities such as Multi-Cultural Events-Japanese Student and American Exchange Program with Japanese Orphanage.

The program was titled Friendship On Wheels Program, that consists of the Japanese Orphanage teaching the American children how to ride a unicycle as well as participated in the exchanged of the American and Japanese games and foods. The American children participated in the Japanese annual parade -- first time to do so in Misawa, Japan history. The event was very excited, fun and memorable. She believes that we can't change the whole world, but we can touch the lives that we are around. After all, these children are the next generation. She believes that whatever we instilled in our children today, will be the outcome of our tomorrow.

In 2006, she became a Breast Cancer overcomer, and an Advocate. She decided to do research and surveyed on Breast Cancer Prevention/Awareness. She was horrified about the lack of knowledge women knew about this disease. She felt some relief of how a large number of this disease can be prevented if people were better educated and well informed on this disease. She also felt a sense of urgency to inform, educate and be available to assist those in need whenever possible. She participated in the Avon Walk for Breast Cancer Research Fundraiser, in two days she walked 39 and half miles, while raising a total of $1,800 for the cause. She found that when the information about Breast Cancer was presented in a positive way, then they are more willing and able to understand it better, accept it and follow through on the preventions.

This was the start of her Annual Breast Cancer Prevention/Awareness Workshop. This has been a very personal and motivational for her as well as a successful journey to write a positive Breast Cancer plays, skits, set up props, created and presented workshops on Breast Cancer Prevention/Awareness for several Churches and Women Conferences throughout the surrounding areas.

The community, churches, businesses and the surrounding area has rally around this annual event. They donated their time, talents, money, free food, door prices, and coupons to help bring awareness to this deadly disease. Her workshops presentations included creating a warm, inviting and friendly atmosphere. Her workshops have provided a platform for breast cancer survivors to share their testimonies to help motivate others to continue to stay in the fight on this disease. She has partner up with several organizations in order to obtain updated resources and materials for her workshops. The organizations included are (abcd) after breast cancer diagnosis, ABC's of Breast Cancer Early Detection, American Cancer Society, Susan G. Komen for the Cure and Avon Walk for Breast Cancer and Cape Fear Cancer Center. All the information resources and materials received from the organizations was included in the table arrangement with breast cancer materials, gift bags, a short film of breast cancer survivor stories, and a very successful skit that she wrote into the presentation titled (Girls Night Out-Share A Story and Change a Life).

The cast included a group of women that are breast cancer survivors and or supporters to help spread the word about this disease. Towards the end of the skit they do an introduction of the cast and a short testimony of their bout with breast cancer. She concluded the workshops with two large pink and white beach type quiz beach balls. The two balls are covered with pink paper butterflies with breast cancer question written on the inside of each butterfly. Each of the question is true/false. The balls are passed throughout the room and where ever it stops, the true/false question began. The audience are informed ahead of time to please pay close attention to what is being said in the skit or play because that is where the answers are! At the end of the workshop the audience are gifted with a bag of goodies, filled with breast cancer pamphlets, books, pens, packages, books marks, door hangers, key chain, and any other kind of resources, materials and items use to get the information out.

As she walks this spiritual journey, she feels blessed beyond imagination. Janice often finds herself in total amazement, when she's in the presence of God, as His peace filled her whole being. She's very appreciative for those moments. When she looks at the world we live in today, she sees signs of the end-times and recognizes that we all are servants of the Lord, fighting this spiritual war. She knows that God is getting her ready for the next level in her life. As He nurtures and prepares her for the next chapter, she shall stand boldly on His word "be ye ready at all time" and like a true soldier, she believes that, you don't give God instructions, you just report for duty! Amen!!

Index

A

abundance, 106, 177
anger, 23, 28, 81, 245

B

bitter, 321
blessings, 20, 258
blood, 4, 62, 108, 291, 312
bondage, 95, 104

C

Christ, 63, 73, 96, 195, 204–5, 209, 272
corruption, 95, 104–5

D

death, 30, 35, 40, 62, 115–16, 160, 190, 213, 224–25, 229, 247, 284, 313, 317, 319
distress, 137

E

encourage, 24, 31
eternal life, 16, 55
excess, 145, 157
extortion, 157

F

fear, 127, 162–63, 250
fools, 81, 164, 272, 280, 318
forgive, 304
fornication, 72, 77, 106, 166, 191, 198, 218, 228, 298

G

generations, 58
glory, 6, 126, 233, 281, 324–25

H

heart, 33, 140, 173, 231, 300, 310
holy, 121
hope, 126–27, 134

I

iniquity, 155, 198

L

liar, 43, 185
love, 18, 23, 25, 27, 127, 149, 162, 185, 235, 334

O

oily, 139, 171, 204

P

peace, 86, 119, 171, 271, 278, 324, 338
persecution, 204, 235, 282
perseverance, 120
perverse, 98, 111
poverty, 21–23, 207, 236
prudent, 248–49

R

relationship, 64–65

righteousness, 32, 119, 124, 222, 235, 303, 327–28

S

sheep, 100, 108, 291
sickness, 83, 233
sins, 2, 8–9, 11, 20–23, 28–31, 33–34, 39–40, 43, 50, 53, 61, 63, 65–66, 97, 124
spirit, 89, 102, 140, 151, 284, 311, 314
steal, 172, 277, 291
strongholds, 14
supplication, 120, 323
sword, 34, 292, 312

T

temptation, 21, 152
tongue, 292
trespass, 230, 297
trust, 117, 171, 188

U

unbelief, 37, 303
uncleanness, 72, 106, 166, 192, 198, 218, 228

unrighteousness, 308–9

V

vain, 174, 192
vanity, 311
voice, 59, 103, 222

W

weapon, 15, 54
wisdom, 164, 226, 241
witchcraft, 319–20

References

1. "Was Jesus ever angry?," Got Questions Ministries, accessed August 6,2018,[https://www.gotquestions.org/Jesus-angry.html]
2. Life Application Bible: New Living Translation. Wheaton ,IL: Tyndale,1996. Print. [intext parenthetical reference examples: (Life Application Bible ,notes on Evidences & Results of Sanctified Affliction)]

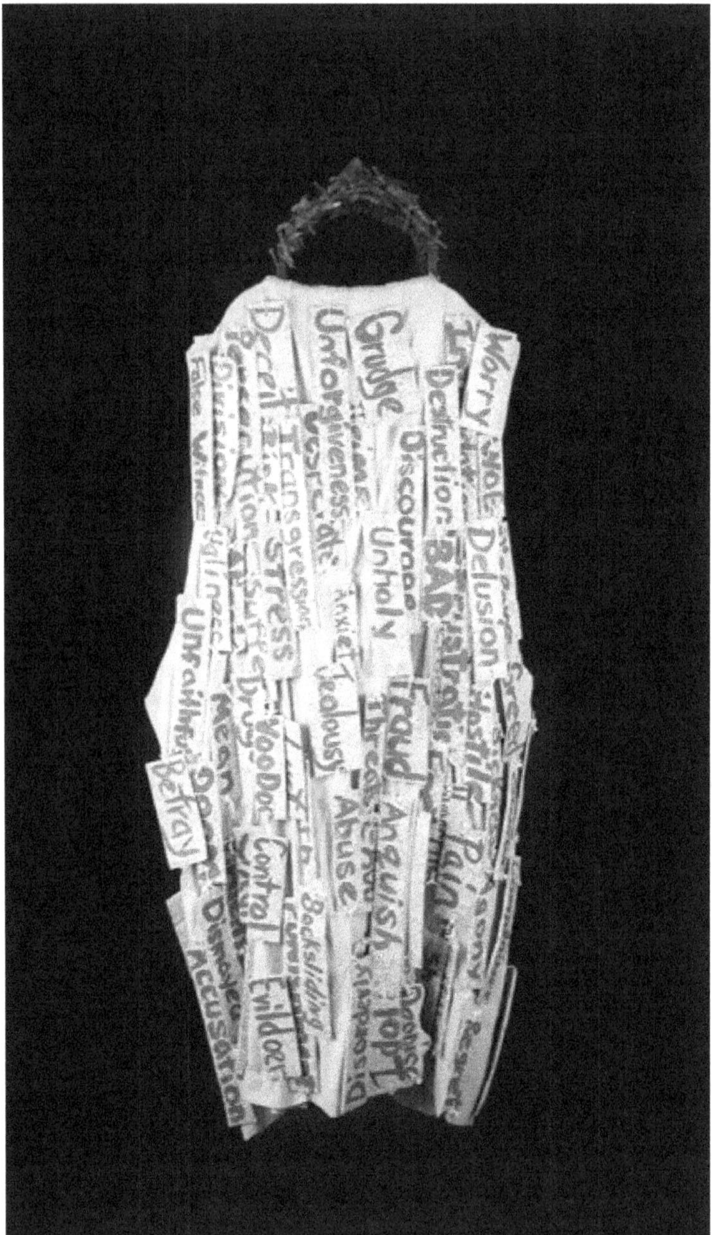
Worry
Destruction
Grudge
Unforgiveness
Deceit
Transgression
Discourage
Unholy
Delusion
BAD
Stress
Anxiety
Jealousy
Fraud
Threats
Unfaithful
Betray
VooDoo
Drugs
Abuse
Anguish
Control
Backsliding
Evildoer
Accusation
Hostile
Pain
Agony

www.ingramcontent.com/pod-product-compliance
Lightning Source LLC
Chambersburg PA
CBHW071259110526
44591CB00010B/716